AF316717

The Path to Enlightenment

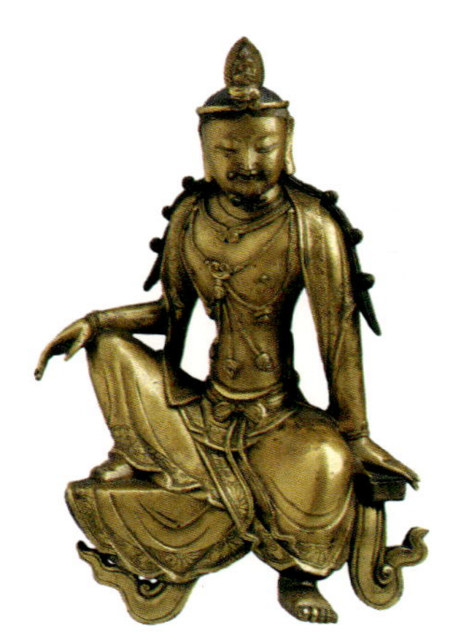

The Path to Enlightenment

✳

MASTERPIECES OF
BUDDHIST SCULPTURE
FROM THE
NATIONAL MUSEUM OF
ASIAN ARTS/MUSÉE GUIMET, PARIS

KIMBELL ART MUSEUM

Fort Worth

The Path to Enlightenment: Masterpieces of Buddhist Sculpture from the National Museum of Asian Arts / Musée Guimet, Paris is published on the occasion of an exhibition organized by the National Museum of Asian Arts / Musée Guimet, Paris, and the Kimbell Art Museum, Fort Worth.

KIMBELL ART MUSEUM, FORT WORTH
5 May–1 September 1996

IDEMITSU MUSEUM OF ARTS, TOKYO
24 September–15 December 1996

The exhibition is supported by an indemnity from the Federal Council on the Arts and the Humanities.

Photographs by Michael Bodycomb, Kimbell Art Museum, except for the following cat. nos.: 1, 2, 5–7, 11–13, 15, 16, 19–23, 34–42, 49, 63, and 66 by Susumu Wakisaka, Idemitsu Museum of Arts; 17, 18, and 45 courtesy of Musée Guimet, Paris. Photographs on page 21 by Jennifer R. Casler.

Translations from the French by Arlette Quervel
Edited by Wendy P. Gottlieb and Mary T. Lees,
    Kimbell Art Museum
Designed by Tom Dawson Graphic Design, Dallas
Printed by The Jarvis Press, Dallas

©1996 by the Kimbell Art Museum, Fort Worth. All rights reserved. This book may not be reproduced, in whole or in part, in any form (beyond that copying permitted by Sections 107 or 108 of the U.S. Copyright Law and except by reviewers for the public press) without written permission from the publishers.

Published by the Kimbell Art Museum, 3333 Camp Bowie Boulevard, Fort Worth, Texas 76107-2792

ISBN 0-912804-32-7

Library of Congress Catalog Card Number: 96-75653

NOTE TO THE READER
Throughout the text, simplified spellings in the Roman alphabet have been used for words from languages originally written in other scripts. Height only is given for most objects.

COVER:
Head of Jayavarman VII? [cat. 61], detail, Cambodia, Angkor?, 12th–13th century, Musée Guimet, Paris

BACK COVER:
Seated Buddha Amida [cat. 51], Japan, Late Heian period, 12th century, Musée Guimet, Paris

Contents

To house his important collections illustrating the great religions of Egypt, classical antiquity, and the Asian world, the industrialist Émile Guimet built a museum that he financed largely by himself and which was inaugurated in Paris in 1889 by Sadi Carnot, president of the French Republic. Guimet was very interested in Buddhism, particularly the Buddhism of Japan, which he first encountered during his 1876 trip around the world. He brought back numerous works from Japan, and these were placed on exhibit first at the 1878 Paris World's Fair and later in a special section of his museum. Guimet was particularly sensitive to the message of tolerance emanating from Buddhism at a time when, in his opinion, Europe was falling prey to aggressive ideologies. Therefore, on 27 June 1898, in the presence of important political figures such as Georges Clémenceau and scientific luminaries such as Louis Pasteur, Guimet asked a lama to hold a ceremony in the museum library, entitled: *"Invocation to Cakya Mouni and all Buddhas to ask them to inspire love and mercy to all human beings."*

Following Guimet's death in 1918, the Asian vocation of the Musée Guimet came more and more to the foreground, and the religious overtones yielded to the quest to collect artworks that could best illustrate the great Asian civilizations of the past. That is why the Musée Guimet began to welcome the archaeological finds of French expeditions and important excavation sites in Asia. During the 1930s, the Musée Guimet received the collections of the Musée Indochinois, which included a remarkable set of Khmer sculptures. In 1945, the decision was made to change the name Musée Guimet to National Museum of Asian Arts. Works dating from the Egyptian period and from Greco-Roman antiquity left the Musée Guimet to go to the Musée du Louvre. In return, the Musée Guimet received the rich Asian collections from the Louvre, including a number of Chinese and Japanese Buddhist pieces. Today, the National Museum of Asian Arts / Musée Guimet is known worldwide for the richness and wide scope of its collections, which become each day more important thanks to generous donations and acquisitions.

Since Émile Guimet never anticipated such a rich collection when he had his museum built, construction has been required at regular intervals to gain new space. Thus, the internal structure of the building, after numerous transformations, has become confusing and storage space and areas to welcome the public are scarce. For this reason, the decision was reached to completely renovate the museum. The collection, therefore, has left the building for a period of two and one-half years (from February 1996 to fall 1998) to allow the addition of a bilevel basement and to completely restructure all internal spaces. This extensive operation follows the renovation of the Louvre, whose Asian collections, as we indicated earlier, are now housed in the Musée Guimet. The French architects Henri and Bruno Gaudin, winners of an international architectural competition, will be in charge of the renovation work until the museum's inauguration, anticipated to take place in late 1998 or early 1999. Paris will then have a museum worthy of the prestigious Asian collections that, over time, have found their way to the building constructed by Émile Guimet.

Even though the Musée Guimet soon ceased to focus mainly on the history of religions, the interest in Buddhism never waned. Émile Guimet was especially attracted to the temples of Japan, which throughout the centuries have kept alive a tradition born in India around the middle of the first millennium B.C. Guimet's successors, following the archaeological explorations and expeditions by Paul Pelliot in Central Asia, the French Archaeological Delegation in Afghanistan, the work at the site of Angkor, and the explorations of men such as Jouveau-Dubreuil, placed more emphasis on ancient Buddhism and its first artistic manifestations. Indian and Gandharan Buddhism were already present in Central Asia in the first centuries A.D., reaching an extraordinary peak in the China of the Six Dynasties (220–589) and the Tang dynasty (618–907). Next, Korea and Japan welcomed the teachings of "Cakya Mouni" and the great lessons of Mahayana Buddhism. During the first centuries A.D., following the development of trade with the Roman world, Indian merchants awaited favorable monsoon winds and brought the products of Southeast Asia back to India, spreading the teachings of their native country over vast new territories. Just like Hinduism, Buddhism also had a major influence on the life of the Indianized kingdoms of Southeast Asia. At the end of the twelfth century, Jayavarman VII, the last great ruler of Angkor, went so far as to transform his kingdom into a huge mandala articulated around his own image as a representation of a compassionate bodhisattva.

To summarize, one may divide the Asian world into two sections: on the one hand, the Indianized countries, strongly impregnated by the Indian traditions, and on the other, the countries that, during their formative years, maintained close links with the great Chinese tradition—its calligraphy, its classics, the cult of the ancestors, and Confucianism. Buddhism, however, with its philosophy and its important lesson concerning the vacuousness of things, became, especially during the fourth and fifth centuries A.D., one of the great cultural components of all countries from India to Japan. By selecting a small number of quality works from our collection, we wish to illustrate this important phenomenon of unity, whose agents—monks, pilgrims, and merchants—traveled the difficult roads followed by the caravans of Central Asia or took to the seas, braving the storms and dangerous waterways of Southeast Asia. It is via these land and sea routes, for which the works shown in this exhibition serve as milestones, that some of the greatest concepts of Indian thought—the cycles of renewal or the feeling that things are impermanent in an illusory world—spread from India to Japan. Thanks to the cult objects traveling along these great routes, the artists found the sources of inspiration that, in spite of the original characteristics of each region, contributed to the similarities between the religious art of Asian countries.

We hope that this collection of works, which is now able to travel thanks to the renovation of the Musée Guimet, shall stand, just like the objects carried long ago by pilgrims and ambassadors, as a shining testament to the great religious and artistic currents that have enriched the various countries of ancient Asia.

•

J E A N - F R A N Ç O I S   J A R R I G E
Conservateur général
National Museum of Asian Arts/Musée Guimet, Paris

When it was first learned that the Musée Guimet would be closing for renovations, the Kimbell Art Museum's director, Dr. Edmund P. Pillsbury, and chief curator, Joachim Pissarro, initiated discussions with Dr. Jean-François Jarrige, conservateur général of the Musée National des Arts Asiatiques-Guimet. Given that the strength of the Kimbell's Asian collection is Buddhist sculpture—the earliest acquisition, made in 1965, was a late-eighth-century bronze *Maitreya* from Prakhon Chai—and that the Musée Guimet's renowned collections began with the Buddhist sculptures brought back from Japan by Émile Guimet in 1876, the Kimbell was pleased to have the opportunity to develop a loan exhibition that would illustrate the evolution and dissemination of Buddhist sculpture from its origins in north central India in the first century throughout the rest of Asia—some ten countries—over the course of nearly two thousand years. The focus on Buddhist sculpture arose from a desire to concentrate on a subject that would make a contribution to general knowledge while highlighting a particularly important facet of the Musée Guimet's encyclopedic collections. There was no interest on the part of the Kimbell or the Musée Guimet in duplicating the 1975 *Rarities of the Musée Guimet* exhibition organized by The Asia Society, in New York, which featured a broad survey of Asian art expressed in a variety of media.

The aim of the exhibition was to select from the French national collection's extensive holdings only the very best examples of Buddhist sculpture representing various cultures, periods, and styles. The selection includes works that were acquired over one hundred years ago as well as a number of significant additions to the collections in recent years. Among its corpus of Asian sculpture, the Guimet's Cambodian material is unsurpassed; therefore, we are pleased to be able to feature in the exhibition nine outstanding examples, including what is undoubtedly one of the most exquisite pieces of Cambodian stone sculpture, the late-twelfth-century Bayon-style *Kneeling Tara* [cat. 62]. Not only does the exhibition showcase the breadth and quality of the Guimet's collection, but the wide range of materials employed—stone, stucco, wood, and precious metals—and the span of time represented—the first through the mid-nineteenth century—demonstrate the richness and variety of Buddhist sculpture and the enduring legacy of Buddhism in Asia.

An undertaking of this magnitude could not have been accomplished without the unstinting efforts of many people.

At the Musée Guimet, Dr. Jarrige was most gracious and generous in granting access to the collections on more than one occasion and approving our proposed selection of sculptures. The curatorial staff of the Musée Guimet kindly contributed the excellent catalogue entries on very short notice; they are listed by name at the beginning of the catalogue section. Pierre Cambon coordinated all aspects of the project for the Musée Guimet—a daunting task—from the photography of the objects and the compilation of the catalogue entries to the condition checking and packing of the objects in Paris. He worked with boundless energy and fortitude to see the exhibition through to its successful installation at the Kimbell.

Were it not for the talents and dedication of my colleagues at the Kimbell Art Museum this exhibition and catalogue could not have been realized in such a short period of time. Many people worked tirelessly in the preparation of the catalogue manuscript. Wendy P. Gottlieb, Kimbell Art Museum editor and assistant director for public affairs, carefully edited the book and was ably assisted by Mary T. Lees. The design and production of the catalogue were undertaken by Tom Dawson, design consultant for the Kimbell Art Museum. Michael Bodycomb, photographer for the Kimbell Art Museum, working under constraints of time and often in less than favorable conditions, managed to provide us with excellent images. Beth Figgers, curatorial assistant, compiled the bibliography. The Kimbell Art Museum's registrar, Anne Adams, coordinated the transportation of the objects and prepared the application for the federal indemnity. Throughout, the constant encouragement, support, and faith of the Kimbell Art Museum's director, Dr. Pillsbury, enabled me to carry out the task at hand and speaks volumes for his commitment to exhibiting non-Western art at the Kimbell.

I wish to express my profound gratitude to all of these exceptional individuals for their knowledge, expertise, and perseverance, without which this exhibition would not have become a reality.

•

JENNIFER R. CASLER
Curator for Asian and Non-Western Art
Kimbell Art Museum

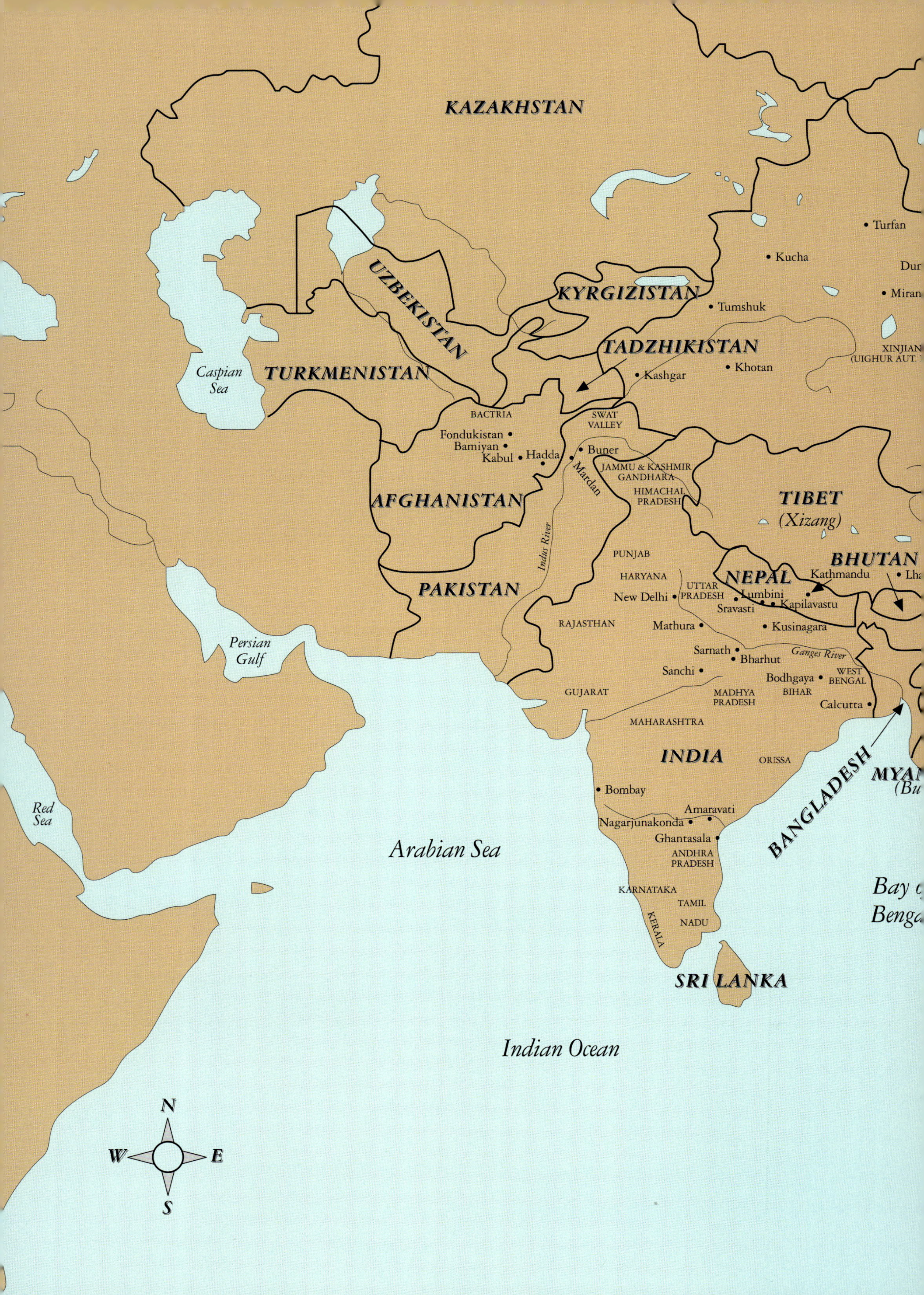

KAZAKHSTAN
Turfan
Kucha
Dur
Miran
UZBEKISTAN
KYRGIZISTAN
Tumshuk
XINJIAN
(UIGHUR AUT.
TADZHIKISTAN
Caspian
Sea
TURKMENISTAN
Kashgar
Khotan
BACTRIA
SWAT
VALLEY
Fondukistan
Bamiyan
Kabul
Hadda
Buner
Mardan
JAMMU & KASHMIR
GANDHARA
HIMACHAL
PRADESH
TIBET
(Xizang)
AFGHANISTAN
Indus River
PUNJAB
BHUTAN
HARYANA
NEPAL
Kathmandu
Lha
PAKISTAN
New Delhi
UTTAR
PRADESH
Lumbini
Kapilavastu
Sravasti
Kusinagara
RAJASTHAN
Mathura
Sarnath
Ganges River
Sanchi
Bharhut
WEST
BENGAL
Persian
Gulf
GUJARAT
MADHYA
PRADESH
Bodhgaya
BIHAR
Calcutta
MAHARASHTRA
INDIA
ORISSA
BANGLADESH
MYAN
(Bu
Red
Sea
Bombay
Amaravati
Nagarjunakonda
Ghantasala
ANDHRA
PRADESH
Arabian Sea
KARNATAKA
TAMIL
NADU
Bay o
Benga
KERALA
SRI LANKA
Indian Ocean
N
W   E
S

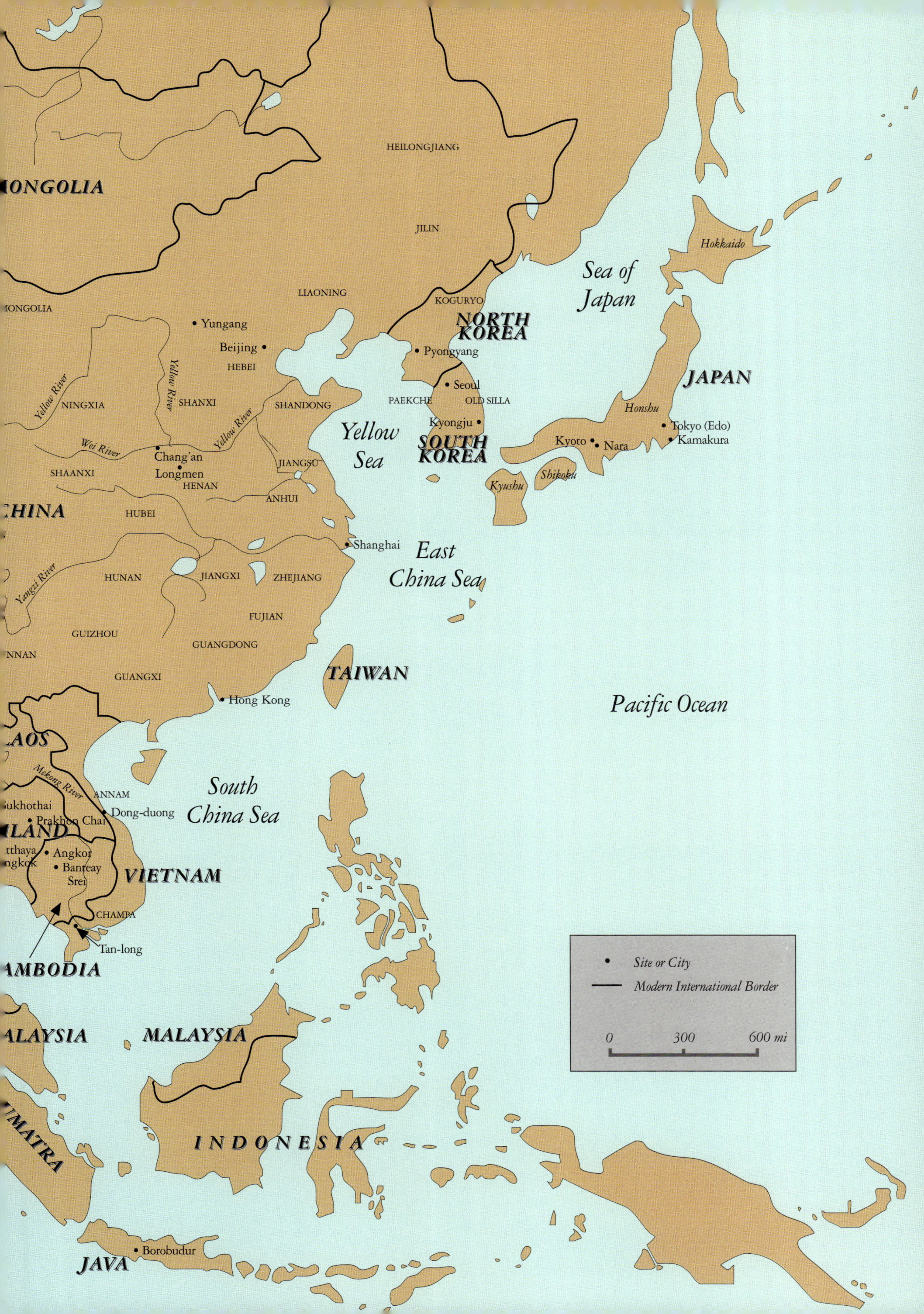

MONGOLIA
MONGOLIA
HEILONGJIANG
JILIN
LIAONING
KOGURYO
NORTH KOREA
Pyongyang
Sea of Japan
Hokkaido
Yungang
Beijing
HEBEI
Yellow River
Yellow River
NINGXIA
SHANXI
SHANDONG
Yellow River
Seoul
PAEKCHE
OLD SILLA
SOUTH KOREA
JAPAN
Honshu
Tokyo (Edo)
Kamakura
Kyoto
Nara
Wei River
SHAANXI
Chang'an
Longmen
HENAN
JIANGSU
Kyongju
Yellow Sea
Kyushu
Shikoku
ANHUI
CHINA
HUBEI
Yangzi River
HUNAN
JIANGXI
ZHEJIANG
Shanghai
East China Sea
FUJIAN
GUIZHOU
GUANGDONG
NNAN
GUANGXI
TAIWAN
Hong Kong
Pacific Ocean
AOS
Mekong River
Sukhothai
Prakhon Chai
ANNAM
Dong-duong
South China Sea
LAND
tthaya
ngkok
Angkor
Banteay Srei
VIETNAM
CHAMPA
Tan-long
AMBODIA
South China Sea
ALAYSIA
MALAYSIA
INDONESIA
MATRA
JAVA
Borobudur
Site or City
Modern International Border
0
300
600 mi

For more than 2,000 years Buddhism has played a pivotal role in serving to link the varied ethnic cultures of Asia and in providing the inspiration for many of the greatest icons of Asian art. From its inception in northeast India in the sixth century B.C., the Buddhist faith was steadily transmitted across the sands of time and the seas of change by merchants and emissaries as well as pilgrims and missionaries, to the far reaches of the Asian world. Throughout East and Southeast Asia, Buddhism served as a major cultural force and in its long history experienced both prosperity and suppression. Although Buddhism is now virtually extinct in the country of its origin, in Nepal it exists peacefully alongside Hinduism; in Japan it has been woven into the fabric of society and survives aesthetically in the arts of Zen Buddhism; in Tibet the mystical form of Tantric (esoteric) Buddhism is still practiced; and in Burma (Myanmar), Sri Lanka, and Thailand the more conservative tradition of Theravada Buddhism continues to be the dominant faith. The triumph of the Buddhist faith can be variously attributed to the support of imperial patronage, the universal appeal of salvation obtainable to all those who seek to break the cycle of rebirth, and its ability to adapt to different cultures and assimilate their native beliefs.

The history of Asian art would indeed be much poorer without the contribution of Buddhist sculpture. Indian models provided the basis for style and iconography, which were subsequently communicated, interpreted, and reformulated from one ethnic region to the next. Ultimately, each culture that embraced the faith created a vocabulary imbued with its own unique artistic traditions, resulting in a vast corpus of Buddhist art exhibiting a rich variety of styles expressed through a wide range of media. Despite ethnic and stylistic diversity, the Buddhist imagery of Asia shares a common design in its ability to convey to its devotees a tangible expression of the spiritual serenity that can only be achieved through transcendence of the material world.

•

Buddhism shared with other religious developments in India the common belief in rebirth or transmigration, whereby a person's life was one in a series, with each life conditioned by the acts or deeds (karma) performed in a previous existence. Accumulated karma, good or bad, determined one's next rebirth; pain and suffering were inherent in the process: birth, old age, sickness, and death. The ultimate goal was to achieve nirvana (the extinction of all desires), whereby perfected knowledge is attained and the painful cycle of rebirths transcended. A bodhisattva is one who is striving towards enlightenment before reaching nirvana.

In keeping with the belief in rebirth, the Buddha was a bodhisattva who had passed through many lives, performing virtuous deeds before his final incarnation. Although stories of his life were soon to be mingled with myth, the Buddha legend begins with a historical founder, who, seeking release from the endless cycle of rebirths, achieved enlightenment and preached the path of salvation to his followers. The dates for the life of the historical Buddha are generally accepted to be 563–483 B.C. He was born a prince, Siddhartha Gautama, of the Shakya tribe of Kapilavastu in what is today the southern region of Nepal. His father, Suddhodana, was chief of the tribe. His conception and birth were miraculous. His mother, Queen Maya, dreamed of a white, six-tusked elephant who entered her womb; ten months later at the Lumbini grove, as she held the branch of a sala tree that bent down towards her, she gave birth to the child painlessly from her right side. After being received and bathed by the gods, he took seven steps to the north and declared his cosmic nature.

He was taken back to Kapilavastu, where a week later his mother died from joy and went to heaven. The thirty-two major and eighty minor signs of a supernatural being (*lakshanas*) were present on his body, and a royal guru predicted that he would become the Buddha. He was given the name Siddhartha, which means "he whose purpose is accomplished." His father, fearing the loss of a son and heir, attempted to shield him from encountering the pain and suffering in the world by keeping him surrounded by comfort within the palace walls. The boy was given a traditional education and was trained in the martial arts. In time, he married his cousin Yasodhara, who bore him a son, Rahula. Despite his father's efforts to protect him, the prince eventually ventured from the palace on four occasions and witnessed in succession an old man, a sick man, a corpse, and a wandering monk. Realizing his destiny, Siddhartha renounced his material life and during the night left his sleeping wife to go out in search of the truth. Once well beyond the palace walls, he cut off his hair and beard, discarded his princely attire and jewelry, and donned the simple robes of a monk.

In the course of his search, he encountered various religious teachers of the time, meditated for a period of six years, and engaged in severe fasting with five ascetics. Dissatisfied with austere methods, he broke his fast and traveled alone to Bodhgaya (in present-day Bihar), where he sat beneath a bodhi tree to meditate until he attained enlightenment. During Siddhartha's meditation, the god of Death, Mara, tried to tempt him in order to protect his own kingdom of death and rebirths. Mara attempted physical assault, sensual temptation by his daughters, the unleashing of a violent storm, and destruction by his army, but was unsuccessful. Siddhartha finally called the earth to witness both his victory over Mara and his ensuing enlightenment by touching the ground with his outstretched right hand; the earth trembled in approval and Mara fled.

Following this, the twenty-nine-year-old Siddhartha, now the Buddha (the Enlightened One), called Shakyamuni (Sage of the Shakyas), continued to meditate for seven weeks during which time he was sheltered from a severe storm by the serpent king Muchalinda, who protected him by coiling his body around the Buddha and spreading his hood above him like a canopy. The Buddha then journeyed to the Deer Park in Sarnath, where he encountered the five ascetics, who, hearing him preach his first sermon, became his first disciples. In this first sermon, in which he "set in motion the Wheel of the Law" (*Dharmachakra*), the Buddha taught that the world is illusory, impermanent, and painful, and that the cause of all human suffering is desire, which must be suppressed in order to escape the endless cycle of rebirths and achieve nirvana. To do this, one must follow the Eightfold Path: right intention, right opinion, right speech, right concentration, right mindfulness, right action, right effort, and right livelihood. The morals and discipline of a monk were required to develop the karma that leads to enlightenment and the end of rebirths.

After a time he returned to Kapilavastu, where he succeeded in converting members of his family to the faith, including his father, his son, his childhood friend Ananda, and his half-brother Nanda. He spent the rest of his life wandering and preaching throughout northeastern India in Bihar and Uttar Pradesh, ordaining converts who wished to be monks, and performing miracles. At the age of eighty he decided it was time to die and chose to go to Kusinagara, in the state of the Malla tribe, who were neighbors and kin to the Shakyas. After taking a meal and bathing in a river, he went into a grove and lay down on a couch prepared by his disciples under a pair of sala trees, went into a trance, and died. The physical death of Buddha, called *Mahaparinirvana* (that which follows the great nirvana), signifies his final release from the cycle of rebirths.

The Buddha did not consider himself to be a divine figure or the founder of a religion; however, the simple message he preached appealed to his followers, who were seeking liberation in a time of instability and change. Buddhism was a reaction against the long-established caste system, the hegemony of the Brahman priests, and those who, opposing the authority of the Brahmans, practiced strict asceticism as a way to salvation. The Buddha taught that an individual could escape the cycle of rebirths through meditation and benevolent conduct, without the intervention of priests and without engaging in severe austerities.

This early form of Buddhism, called Hinayana (the Little Vehicle), or, in the southern Pali language, Theravada (the Way of the Elders), stressed the teachings and ethics of the historical Buddha Shakyamuni, which required his disciples to live as monks and to concentrate solely on reaching nirvana. Theravada Buddhists believed that Shakyamuni was last in a series of twenty-four past Buddhas. In Buddhist art, Theravada subject matter focuses on images of Shakyamuni and narrative scenes of his previous lives as a bodhisattva (*jatakas*).

Sometime in the first century A.D., developments in the Buddhist religion resulted in the formation of a new sect called Mahayana (the Great Vehicle). In Mahayana, the Buddha Shakyamuni became an eternal supreme being, a god, who was now part of an expanded pantheon of past and future Buddhas, as well as numerous attendant bodhisattvas. These bodhisattvas were enlightened beings who indefinitely postponed their own final nirvana in order to assist mankind on the path to salvation, which was now available to everyone, monks and laymen. In time, many of these Buddhas and bodhisattvas soon developed their own cult followings, which in turn significantly influenced and expanded the subject matter of Buddhist art. Among the most popular are: Maitreya, the Buddha of the future age (as a potential Buddha he is also portrayed as a bodhisattva who presides over the Tushita Heaven); Amitabha, the Buddha of Infinite Life or Light, who presides over the Pure Land, or Western Paradise; Avalokiteshvara, the bodhisattva of compassion; and Manjushri, the bodhisattva of wisdom.

A third sect, Vajrayana (the Diamond Path), alternately referred to as Tantric or esoteric Buddhism, emerged around the seventh century as a result of the development of *tantras*, texts involving ritual and meditational techniques that were used as a means of attaining nirvana. Through the use of *dharanis* (incantations), *mandalas* (cosmic diagrams), and *mudras* (ritual gestures), the adept meditates on one particular aspect of the Buddha to achieve union with him, shortening the process of attaining enlightenment. Rather than relying on the aid of a bodhisattva, as in Mahayana, this system of esoteric Buddhism required the interaction of a guru, a teacher who already possessed strong spiritual powers, to reach a state of nirvana. In the reconfigured Vajrayana pantheon, there were four cosmic Buddhas associated with the four directions—Amoghasiddhi (north), Ratnasambhava (south), Aksobhaya (east), and Amitabha (west)—and a central, supreme Buddha, Vairocana. Five bodhisattvas were the spiritual emanations of these Buddhas and were provided with female consorts. Other deities, some of them terrifying, were included in each Buddha's "family," resulting in a highly elaborated Buddhist cosmology.

•

The beginnings of Buddhist art emerged in the third century B.C. Legend has it that a Buddha image was fashioned during the Buddha's lifetime by King Udayana of Kausambi, who, distraught over the Buddha's absence from earth as he went to the heavens to preach, had a statue of the Buddha made in sandalwood. Artistic evidence, however, clearly demonstrates that in early Buddhist art the Buddha was represented by symbols. By the second century B.C. narrative reliefs on the famous stupas at Sanchi and Bharhut in Madhya Pradesh depicted didactic stories of the Buddha's life, past and present, with the Buddha represented symbolically. The most important early symbols were: a footprint (the Buddha); the empty throne (royalty); a standing woman (his birth); the bodhi tree (enlightenment); the wheel (first sermon at the Deer Park); and a stupa (his death). The expansion of the Buddhist faith and resultant imagery can be attributed to the imperial patronage of the Mauryan emperor Ashoka (272–231 B.C.), who championed the religion through the construction of monuments and the erection of dedicatory pillars throughout India.

Prior to the existence of iconic images of the Buddha, the chief monument of Buddhist worship was the stupa. Based on earlier Hindu burial mounds, a stupa was comprised of a solid domed brick or stone structure (*anda*) set on a low platform, surmounted by a pillar with three umbrellas surrounded by a square railing (*harmika*). The entire structure was enclosed by a stone balustrade (*vedika*) consisting of posts (*stambha*) and crossbars, with four gateways (*torana*) positioned at the cardinal points. Stupas originally served as reliquary mounds for the Buddha's remains and later functioned as tombs for religious teachers, or as containers of relics or other sacred objects. To accrue merit, worshippers would circumambulate the stupa clockwise (*pradaksina*); donors who financed the building of new stupas and maintenance of existing stupas gained merit as well.

The earliest Buddhist imagery was found on the exterior side of the balustrades, posts, and gateways of the stupa, which were elaborately carved with *jatakas* (stories from the former lives of the Buddha) and female fertility images. Later stupas added carved marble panels to cover the body of the stupa itself, such as those at Ghantasala and Nagarjunakonda in the Amaravati region of Andhra Pradesh in the second and third centuries A.D. [cats. 5–7], repeating the same narrative formulas as seen earlier at Sanchi and Bharhut. In addition to the *jatakas*, narrative reliefs most often depicted the eight "Great Miracles," the eight most significant events from the Buddha Shakyamuni's life. Four were singled out in particular: the birth at the Lumbini grove, the enlightenment at Bodhgaya, the first sermon at Sarnath, and the *Mahaparinirvana* at Kusinagara. The remaining four events recounted miracles performed in four cities during the Buddha's lifetime. In the city of Sravasti, the Buddha actually performed seven miracles on one occasion, including walking in the air while emitting flames and water from his body [cat. 18]. Although the eight "Great Miracles" were the most popular narrative motifs, other isolated episodes from the Buddha's life were represented on reliefs, such as the night Siddhartha left the palace in search of the truth, often referred to as "the Great Departure." In a scene such as this, the presence of the Buddha was often symbolized by a sunshade (*chattra*) being held by a servant, indicating the presence of royalty [cat. 6].

Another prevalent subject carved onto the *stambha* were *shalabhanjikas* and *yakshis*, female fertility images. Different types of fertility goddesses were an important component of early Indian nature cults prior to the advent of Buddhism and were eventually assimilated into the symbolic repertoire of Buddhist art. The belief that the touch of a female was capable of making a tree blossom was made implicit in the carving of these young, beautiful, sensuous, female figures. *Shalabhanjika* images generally consisted of a woman and a tree and were carved in innumerable variations. Other examples depicted *yakshis* engaging in various activities, such as trampling demons underfoot, and could include other small figures peering from balconies overhead. The tradition of carving voluptuous female figures on stupa railing pillars continued into the Kushan period, as seen in art from Mathura [cat. 4].

The first appearance of images of the Buddha and bodhisattvas occurred sometime in the first century A.D., during the reign of the Kushan ruler Kaniska I (c. A.D. 100). The Kushans ruled from the first to third centuries in much of northwestern India and the ancient region of Gandhara (parts of present-day Pakistan and Afghanistan). The creation of a Buddha image in human form corresponded to the theological changes taking place in the religion, which ultimately resulted in the formation of the Mahayana sect and subsequently to the layman's need for a devotional image as a spiritual aid.

It was during the Kushan period that the basic repertoire of Buddhist iconography was formulated. *Lakshanas*, auspicious physical attributes or marks on the body of the Buddha indicating his status as a supernatural being, were specified in the early literature. The most important *lakshanas* were: the *ushnisha*, the cranial protuberance on top of the Buddha's head, and the *urna*, the tuft of hair between the eyebrows, both signs of the Buddha's superior wisdom; hands and feet like a net, represented by webbed fingers and toes; and the palms of the hands and soles of the feet marked by wheels. Some attributes were not always consistently followed and certain features became standard that were not actually included on the list, such as earlobes elongated by the weight of heavy princely jewelry, and parallel folds on the neck meant to resemble the upper part of a conch. Some attributes were exclusive to Buddha images, such as the *ushnisha*, while others could also be seen on bodhisattvas.

Another means of identification were *mudras*, or gestures, which also became standardized. The gestures of the Buddha were limited to five: the most common, the gesture of reassurance (*abhayamudra*), in which the right hand is raised with palm usually turned outward; the gesture of meditation (*dhyanamudra*), with the hands in the lap and the palms facing upward, one on top of the other; bestowing charity or blessing (*varadamudra*), with the right hand held down towards the ground and the palm turned outwards; calling the earth to witness (*bhumisparshamudra*), with the right hand touching the ground, the palm turned inward; and the gesture of preaching (*dharmachakramudra*), in which the hands are brought together in front of the chest, the left with palm upward below the right, both having thumb and forefinger touching. Together, the two hands form a circle and symbolically suggest the turning of the wheel.

Two distinct styles of sculpture emerged during the Kushan period, one associated with the region of Gandhara and one with the city of Mathura in north India. Mathura, in present-day Uttar Pradesh, was the second capital of the Kushans and a major center of art production. Making use of

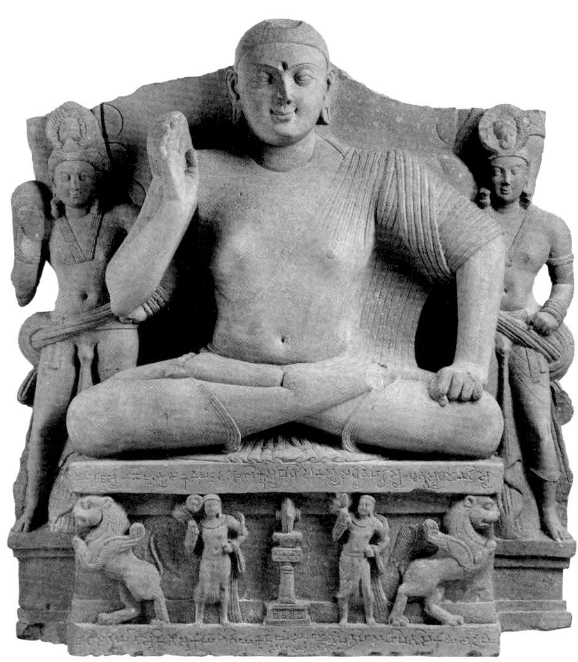

FIG. 1
Seated Kapardin Buddha with Two Attendants, India, Mathura, Kushan period,
1st–2nd century, red sandstone, h. 36¾ in. (93.3 cm).
Kimbell Art Museum, Fort Worth

the local mottled red sandstone, Mathuran art developed from the indigenous Indian artistic traditions found in the earlier reliefs at Bharhut and Sanchi. The standard Mathura-type Buddha was portrayed seated as a traditional yogi [fig. 1], shown either in meditation or preaching, and dressed in the guise of a monk. The thin, diaphanous robe was worn over the left shoulder leaving the right shoulder bare. The sensitive and soft modeling of the flesh gave no hint of the musculature underneath but still endowed the body with a sense of solidity and mass. The hair was smooth like a cap and the cranial bump appeared as a twisted bun or coil of hair (*kaparda*). Sculptures of the Buddha were often carved in the form of a stele and could include other symbols or figures referring to the Buddha's life or exalted status as a universal monarch (*chakravartin*): a halo behind the Buddha's head represented the sun and divinity; attendant figures holding fly whisks (*chauri*) signified royalty, as did a lion throne; and the presence of a wheel was symbolic of his first sermon at Sarnath. Whether seated or standing [cat. 3], Kushan-period *kapardin*-type Buddhas from Mathura, with their wide-open eyes and slightly archaic smile, displayed a very direct attitude towards the viewer.

The second style of Buddhist sculpture was produced in Gandhara between the first and sixth centuries. Carved from gray schist, Gandharan sculptures were iconographically similar but stylistically distinct from their Mathuran counterparts. Gandharan art was heavily influenced by the artistic traditions of the Hellenistic world, most probably as a result of Alexander the Great's colony in Bactria (western Afghanistan). The monastic robes of the Gandharan Buddha covered both shoulders; the thick, heavy folds of drapery were more naturalistically modeled and voluminous. The Apollonian face was smooth and oval-shaped with a straight nose and well-defined eyes shown half-closed as if in a state of meditation. The hair was rendered in wavy lines and the *ushnisha* depicted as a wavy topknot; the *urna* was often conceived as a raised circle between the brows [cat. 18].

Bodhisattva images emerged at the same time as images of the Buddha in both Gandharan and Mathuran art. Sometimes they served as attendants to the Buddha and sometimes they stood alone. Bodhisattvas possessed some of the same superhuman traits as the Buddha, having elongated earlobes and *urna*, and displayed similar *mudra*, but they did not have the *ushnisha*. At first, they were primarily distinguished from images of the Buddha by their secular attire, such as a turban and earrings [cat. 1], a sophisticated coiffure and moustache [cat. 13], and noble robes and jewelry [cat. 14], all alluding to the Buddha's life as prince before reaching enlightenment. Eventually, individual bodhisattvas were also identified by the attributes they held in their hands or symbols worn in their hair.

The tradition of decorating stupas with relief carvings depicting scenes of the life of the Buddha continued during the Kushan period in both Gandhara and in the Ikshvaku kingdom in Andhra Pradesh (central eastern India). In Gandhara, horizontally oriented narrative scenes demarcated by Corinthian capitals were typified by somewhat static compositions reduced to a minimum number of figures [cat. 12]. By comparison, artists in the Mardan region of Gandhara carved in very high relief, almost in the round, creating harmoniously integrated configurations of lively figures in naturalistic poses [cat. 15]. In Andhra Pradesh, the independent style of the Amaravati school was characterized by dense and spatially complex compositions filled with animated yet refined figures [cats. 6, 7]. By the following Gupta period, however, the interest in narrative sculpture had sharply declined as the emphasis on carving various images in the expanded pantheon of Mahayana Buddhas and bodhisattvas increased.

During the rule of the Gupta kings in north and north-central India (A.D. 321–550), the iconographic features cultivated during the Kushan period were codified into a textual as well as visual vocabulary that would serve as a model to all of the various countries to which Buddhism traveled. Certain iconographic traits of the Buddha image remained immutable; he is always shown in the traditional attire of a monk, he is never portrayed with multiple limbs, and he is always represented as eternally youthful. Visual metaphors expressed the Buddha's perfected state of being: he had a face shaped like an egg, eyes shaped like lotus petals, lips full like a ripe mango, the broad shoulders of an elephant, and the tapering torso of a lion. Other typical Gupta-period features were the eyes, now depicted as half-closed as if in meditation; the hair, transformed into a "snail-shell" pattern consisting of short spirals that are ritually curled to the right and cover the more prominent *ushnisha*; and the disappearance of the *urna* between the eyebrows [cat. 9]. A uniform, "classic" style of Buddha was thus perfected and subsequently spread through much of India and beyond.

Mathura continued to be a major center of artistic production. The classic Mathuran Buddha created around the mid-fifth century combined the solid yet plastic forms expressed in Kushan-period sculpture with an increased linearity. The outcome yielded more refined modeling and smooth, flowing volumes. The most typical feature of Mathuran Buddhas was a stylized drapery pattern consisting of cascading pleats delineated into a threadlike surface design [cat. 10]. This stylistic concept was adapted by Mathuran artists from the more naturalistic drapery seen in Gandhara. The Mathuran Buddha, normally a standing figure and over-life-size, maintained a totally frontal and slightly stiff posture, with the right hand raised in the gesture of reassurance and the head framed by a decorative halo.

In addition to Mathura a second artistic center arose in Sarnath, in Uttar Pradesh. The artists here created a Buddha image imbued with an ethereal presence. In comparison to Mathura, the Sarnath Buddha was serenely elegant, with a more graceful body and relaxed posture. The monk's robe covered the entire body and was smoothly modeled as if transparent, with no drapery folds, so that there was little distinction between the fabric and the body underneath. From the Gupta period on, this sensual yet dignified Buddha image had a profound influence on the Buddhist art produced in India and throughout East and Southeast Asia.

By the fourth century the Kushans lost much of their control of Gandhara, and by the early sixth century many Buddhist monuments in Pakistan had been destroyed by the invading White Huns. Despite invasion and persecution, Buddhism continued to flourish in Afghanistan into the eighth century. The most abundant Afghan remains are the late Gandharan stucco sculptures discovered at the Tapa Kalan monastery in Hadda dating to the fourth to fifth century [cats. 19, 20]. Stylistically these images continued to owe a debt to the Hellenistic world. In Gandhara the use of stucco, common from the third century, was believed to have originated in Alexandria. At Fondukistan, between Bamiyan and Kabul, a uniquely mannerist style influenced by post-Gupta Indian sculpture developed in the seventh to eighth century, characterized by suavely elegant and beautifully adorned Buddhas and bodhisattvas [cats. 21–23] fashioned from baked clay and brightly polychromed.

In India, the last significant phase of Buddhist practice occurred during the Pala and Sena dynasties, who ruled eastern India (the present-day states of Bihar, West Bengal, and Bangladesh) from the late eighth to the early thirteenth century. The Pala emperors were Buddhist, and a prodigious amount of art, both Buddhist and Hindu, was produced during their reign. As the Buddhist holy land was located in and around south Bihar, monks from all over Asia made pilgrimages to eastern India to study and visit famous sites. Consequently, the influence of the Pala style on Buddhist art was spread to many Asian countries. By the thirteenth century, towards the end of the Pala period, the destruction of many Buddhist monuments and sculpture during the Muslim invasions in the twelfth century and the subsequent rise of Hinduism as an organized religion served to displace the dominance of the Buddhist faith in India.

Although early Pala art was influenced by the Gupta Sarnath style, visible in the soft modeling of figures and more restrained decoration, Pala artists preferred to emphasize fluid outlines rather than volume. A ninth-century stele of the goddess *Tara* [cat. 11] displays a heaviness and fullness in the figure and slight rigidity of pose that connect it to Gupta art, but the soft modeling of curves and more elaborate rendering of the costume and jewelry link the image to the Pala style. Tara, the female counterpart of Avalokiteshvara, was widely worshipped in eastern India as a protective deity and goddess of great compassion. She commonly holds a blue lotus in the left hand and extends the right hand in the gesture of charity; she was often portrayed with her two attendants, Marici and Ekajata. The cult of Tara was developed by Mahayana and esoteric Buddhists in India, and later in Tibet.

The expanding complexity of imagery and iconographic detail indicative of later Pala art paralleled the development and growing practice of esoteric Buddhism in eastern India. Khasarpana Lokeshvara, the esoteric form of the immensely popular bodhisattva of compassion, Avalokiteshvara, was frequently portrayed in Pala art. In a stele dating to the twelfth century [fig. 2], the elegant proportions, attenuated waistline, richly carved surface decoration, and almost feminine poise of the bodhisattva are hallmarks of the mature Pala style.

•

In the Himalayan kingdoms of Kashmir, Nepal, and Tibet, aesthetic influences traveled back and forth and artistic inspiration from outside cultural regions was assimilated into native traditions. Both Buddhism and Hinduism inspired the art of the Himalayas. As early as the Kushan period, Kashmir was a major center of Buddhist scholarship and continued to be an artistic source for the second propagation of the Buddhist religion in the late tenth and early eleventh century. Located in a valley in northwest India (present-day Jammu and Kashmir), Kashmir provided an important link between India and Central Asia, China, and Tibet. Kashmiri Buddhist bronzes from the seventh century exhibit a combination of the Gandharan and Gupta styles. By the eighth century a Kashmiri style reflecting the growing influence of esoteric Buddhism from Pala India began to develop. In an image of the bodhisattva Avalokiteshvara dating to the eleventh century [cat. 27], the delicate facial features, elongated torso, and abundance of jewelry are a reference to Pala India; the multiarms, elaborate tiara, and flower garland demonstrate Hindu influence; and the pointed nimbus and inlaid silver eyes are characteristic of later Kashmiri bronzes.

Nepal was closest to India culturally as well as geographically. The Licchavis from north India entered the

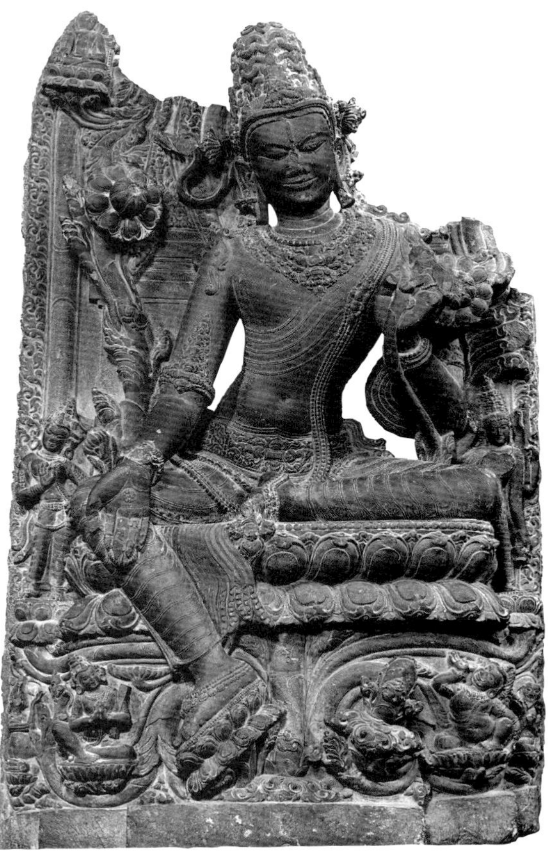

Fig. 2

Bodhisattva Khasarpana Lokeshvara, India, Bengal, 12th century, gray schist, h. 49¼ in. (124.9 cm), Kimbell Art Museum, Fort Worth

Kathmandu Valley in the third century and began an artistic tradition that originally borrowed from Tibet and India and eventually evolved into a distinct Nepali style. Both Hinduism and Buddhism were introduced from India at an early date. The early Buddhist art of Nepal is nearly indistinguishable from Gupta-period bronzes of the sixth and seventh centuries [fig. 3], combining the Sarnath and Mathura idioms. The Gupta influence continued until the tenth century, but by the ninth century the Pala style began to be more dominant in Nepalese sculpture, evident in the increased linear treatment of the body and greater emphasis on ornamentation.

Much of Nepalese art was created by a minority community known as the Newars, who were concentrated in the Kathmandu Valley. The Nepalese Newars were highly skilled and creative metalsmiths who consequently played a prominent role in the art of Tibet. Newari statuary reached its apogee in the thirteenth to the fifteenth century during the early Malla dynasty (1200–1482), and was noted for the use of semiprecious stones as embellishments for crowns and jewelry. Elegant standing bodhisattva images represent the pinnacle of Nepalese figurative sculpture. A thirteenth-century *Manjushri* [cat. 25], the bodhisattva of wisdom, stands in a *tribhanga* (thrice-bent) pose with gracefully swaying hips and exaggerated waist and thighs. The encrusted crown and jewelry are indicative of the Newari penchant for inlay while still exhibiting some restraint. The Nepalese fondness for lavish decoration flourished in the fourteenth century with an exuberance that can still be seen in sculpture of the early nineteenth century [cat. 26].

Buddhism, introduced into Tibet in the seventh century via the auspices of both China and India, was made the state religion in the eighth century but waned during the Buddhist persecutions in 840 and 842. The Buddhist faith met continued resistance until the late tenth century, when changes in political authority brought about a resurgence of the religion. Native Tibetan elements merged with eastern Indian and Kashmiri Buddhist traditions to produce a religious art and culture of remarkable diversity. Tibet has remained to the present a primarily Buddhist country dominated by Lamaism, a form of esoteric Buddhism in which the lama or teacher has enormous power.

Little Tibetan art prior to the tenth century survives. Buddhist art from Pala-period Bihar was the primary source for Tibetan art in the late eleventh to the thirteenth century, by which time Nepali art had begun to inspire Tibetan artists. Newari craftsmen were employed by Tibetan patrons, and the use of inlay was transmitted from Nepal to Tibet. In south and central Tibet, painting and sculpture fol-

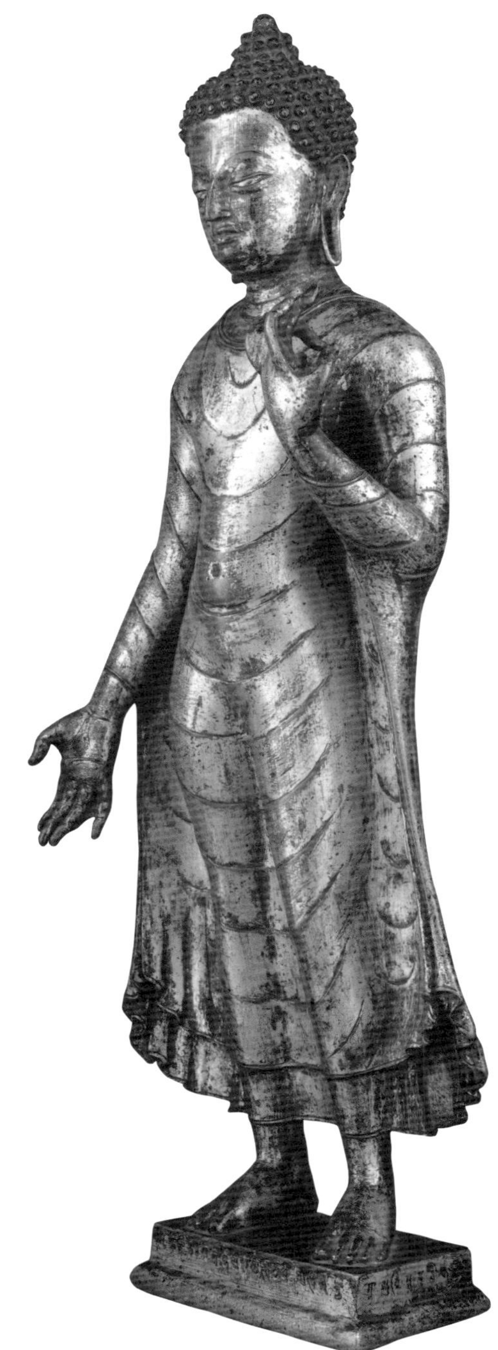

Buddha Shakyamuni, Nepal, Licchavi period, 7th century, gilt copper, h. 19¾ in. (50.2 cm), Kimbell Art Museum, Fort Worth

lowed eastern Indian and Nepalese models. In western Tibet, the influence of Kashmir was strong, due to the importation of Kashmiri-style bronzes into this region, although the presence of the eastern Indian Pala style was not completely absent. The impact of Indian and Kashmiri traditions on the art of western Tibet in the late tenth to the early eleventh century can be seen in an image of *Vajrapani*, the "bearer of lightning" [cat. 28], a popular figure in esoteric Buddhism due to his emblem, the *vajra* (diamond thunderbolt). The delicate floral patterns of the skirt, draped to leave one knee bare, the elegant tiara with fleuron points, and the garland dropping below the knees are all elements that show strong Kashmiri influence [cat. 27]. The elongation of the body with exaggerated waistline and the pose of the figure link the piece to western Tibet.

A fifteenth-century figure of the historical Buddha *Shakyamuni* [cat. 29] displaying the *bhumisparshamudra* demonstrates the continued impact of Pala iconography and style on esoteric art in Tibet. The "earth-touching" pose is typical of Pala art while the *vajra* placed in front of the figure of Shakyamuni connects the sculpture to esoteric Buddhism. The art and culture of Tibet is best known for the practice and preservation of esoteric (Vajrayana) Buddhism. As in Nepal, Tibet had a long history of exercising meditation as a means to bring the practitioner into a mystical union with a chosen divinity representing Buddhahood. A feature common in later Nepalese and Tibetan art was the depiction of deities in stylized sexual union (*yab-yum*). The male is the active means to salvation, and his female counterpart (*prajna*) is wisdom; their symbolic union brings emancipation. In late Tibetan art these esoteric configurations are often realized as multilimbed, multiheaded, and quite fierce [cat. 30].

A distinctive Tibetan style was eventually born out of a mixture of influences, including that of China from an early period. The representations of Buddhist Guardian Kings (Lokapala) in Tibet was strongly marked by Chinese influence in the depiction of their armor, which was a variation of Tang-period Lokapala, such as those from Dunhuang [cats. 34, 35]. In a fifteenth-century *Virupaksa*, the Guardian King of the West [cat. 32], the iconography derives from China but the ornate gilding and use of turquoise inlay firmly establish the piece as Tibetan.

•

The ancient Silk Road played a vital role in the transmission of Buddhism to East Asia, as it was the main conduit of trade and communication between India and China. From late Hellenistic times, silk and other merchandise were transported between the Western world and China, and with the advent of Buddhist missionaries the Silk Road became the route for Buddhist travelers in search of Indian scriptures and for the introduction of Indian and Greco-Roman art forms into China. Roads from India led through Afghanistan, the Swat Valley of Pakistan and Kashmir, to Kashgar, where the Silk Road split into two routes, a northern one through Kucha, Turfan, and Dunhuang, and a southern one that passed through Khotan, Miran, Dunhuang, and finally to Chang'an, the capital of China

during the Han and Tang dynasties. Many of the ancient city-states along these Central Asian routes adopted Buddhism, building monuments, monasteries, and cave temples in the desert, and from there Buddhism entered China. The artistic traditions of Central Asia were varied and preserved a number of styles, sometimes mixed—from India, Gandhara, Kashmir, Iran, Afghanistan, the classical West, and China [cats. 34–37].

Buddhism was introduced into China in the Eastern Han dynasty (A.D. 25–220) and gradually gained acceptance throughout the empire. The fall of the Han in the third century precipitated a temporary loss of confidence in the long-established Confucian order and the imperial mandate of heaven, which resulted in political division and foreign invasion. The instability and uncertainty of the following four centuries cleared the way for Buddhism, which offered an escape from a troubled world. The discipline of the religion appealed to Confucian ethics, while the idea of being reborn into a Buddhist paradise catered to the Taoists' search for immortality. Being a tolerant and adaptable religion, Buddhism was easily assimilated into Chinese culture. During this period the texts of all the major schools from India were translated, and followers of all sects coexisted. The indigenous schools of Chinese Buddhism did not emerge until the Tang dynasty (618–907).

Through the Tang dynasty, Buddhism enjoyed imperial patronage but continually withstood opposition from native Confucianism. In response to the Confucian criticism that Buddhist monks were not obligated to fulfill the duties of filial piety, Chinese Chan Buddhism was conceived. The Chan school taught that the Buddha nature was intrinsic in every person and could be realized through self-cultivation and meditation without withdrawing from the world. In Chan, the lay person could adhere to Buddhist practice while still maintaining the family obligations essential to Confucian morals.

Chinese Buddhism was also distinguished by the development and propagation of Pure Land paradise cults, based in part on the Mahayana belief that multiple Buddhas and bodhisattvas inhabited different paradises. The unstable condition of China in the sixth century generated a desire by many to be reborn in a Buddhist paradise, such as the Tushita Pure Land of the bodhisattva Maitreya or the Western Pure Land of Amitabha Buddha. These Pure Lands offered a haven in which devotees could perfect their karma in order to gain enlightenment. The most popular sect was the Western Pure Land, which stressed meritorious deeds and devotion to Amitabha. The popularity of Pure Land sects was later transmitted from China to Korea and Japan.

From the third to the sixth century the greatest Buddhist monuments were the immense carved and painted cave temple complexes at Yungang (Shanxi province), Longmen (Henan province), and Dunhuang (Gansu province). The earliest caves were established in Dunhuang in A.D. 366. At Yungang, near Datong, the first caves were cut in A.D. 460 under the patronage of the foreign Toba Wei, who ruled China from the late fourth to the early sixth century during the Northern Wei dynasty (386–535). Over a period of thirty years, twenty caves, some enormous, were cut into a soft cliffside and were intricately carved and decorated. The *Colossal Buddha*, nearly fourteen meters high, retained a strong Central Asian influence [fig. 4], but other figures in smaller caves had slimmer bodies and faces, stylishly pleated robes, and leaned slightly forward [fig. 5]. This new sense of movement and stylized linearity—the beginnings of a distinct Chinese style—resulted in an attenuation, even distortion, of features that was further developed at a second group of Toba Wei cave temples to the south at Longmen, near Luoyang, the second Wei capital established in 495 [cat. 38]. Following the Northern Wei, a transitional style emerged during the brief Northern Qi dynasty (550–577) to the north in Hebei province. Sculptures carved in white marble were characterized by a more columnar silhouette with broad shoulders, elegant torsos, and long legs [cat. 39]. The fuller cheeks and generally plump features of Northern Qi figures were later incorporated into Tang aesthetics.

The Tang period marked the ultimate triumph of Buddhism in China, and it was during this dynasty that Buddhist sculpture realized a Chinese mastery of the Indian style. This wholly Chinese style came from India through Central Asia and was perfectly assimilated into the marvelous plasticity of Tang sculpture. Sculpture in the round was perfected during the Tang; figures were fleshy, sensuous, and tactile, their sumptuous garments carved to accentuate the contours of the body, with flowing scarves and clinging ropes of beads to emphasize curves [fig. 6]. Bodhisattvas, attendant figures, and fierce guardians stood or sat in a relaxed *tribhanga* stance, the weight on one hip [cats. 34, 35]. This International Tang style became the ultimate model for the transmission of Buddhist sculpture to the rest of East Asia.

Buddhism in China survived persecutions in the mid-fifth century and again in the late sixth century, but after the mid-Tang Buddhist proscription of 843–45 the religion fell from imperial favor and was once again suspect. What followed was a marked period of slow decline and transformation of Buddhism in China, although it never completely

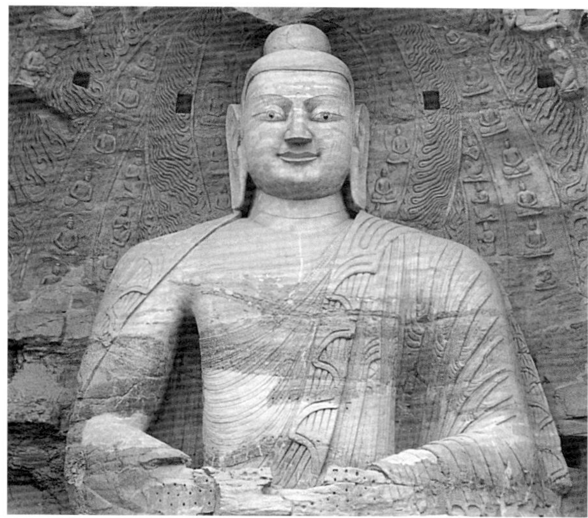

FIG. 4
Colossal Buddha (detail), China, Shanxi province, Yungang, cave 20, Northern Wei dynasty, 5th century, stone, h. 45 ft. (13.7 m)

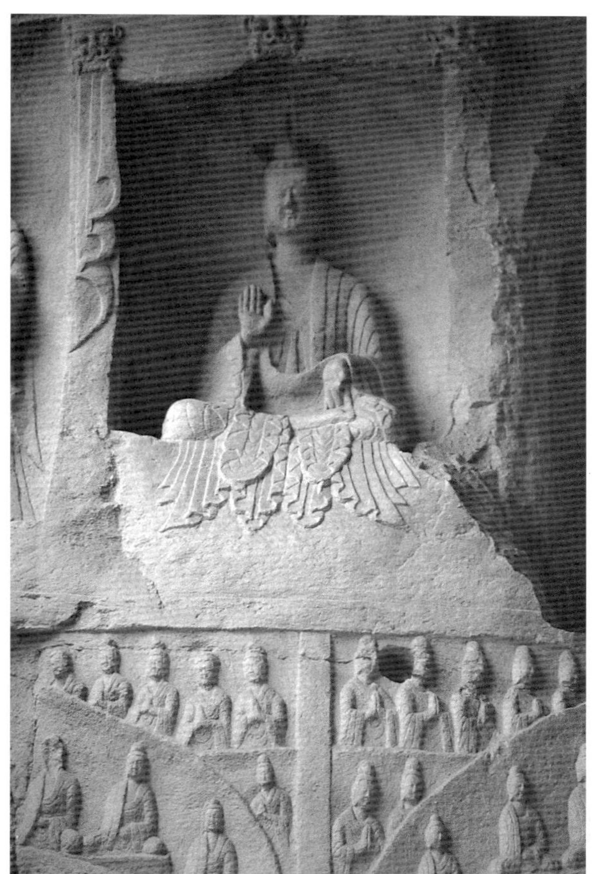

FIG. 5
Seated Bodhisattva, China, Shanxi province, cave temple at Yungang, Northern Wei dynasty, 5th century, stone

disappeared. After the tenth century, Buddhist art existed on a reduced scale, and the more economical wood and stucco replaced stone as a medium for sculpture. Many life-size wooden statues of the ever-popular bodhisattva of compassion, Avalokiteshvara (Chinese, Guanyin) were made in the

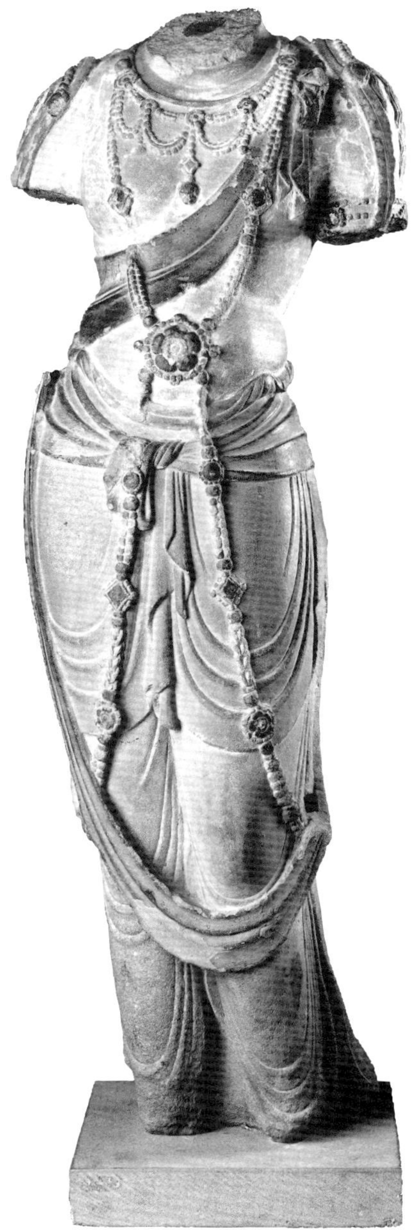

Bodhisattva Torso, China, Tang dynasty, c. 775–800, gray limestone, traces of gesso and pigments, h. 37 in. (94 cm), Kimbell Art Museum, Fort Worth

Song dynasty (960–1279) [cat. 42]. These Song bodhisattvas are stylistically related to their Tang prototypes but are somewhat stilted and far less animated. The Chan and Pure Land sects survived into the Ming dynasty (1368–1644), and the Qing (1644–1911) Manchu emperors espoused the religion, particularly Tibetan Lamaism, commissioning a large number of Sino-Tibetan Buddhist images [cat. 33].

The enthusiasm with which China embraced Buddhism led to its subsequent transmission to Korea and Japan; consequently China, not India, influenced the Buddhist thought and artistic styles of its neighbors. The traditional date for the introduction of Buddhism into Korea is A.D. 372, during the Three Kingdoms period (?37 B.C.

–A.D. 668), after which the religion spread gradually through Korea until, with the unification of the country under the Unified Silla Kingdom in A.D. 668, it was firmly adopted as a state religion. As in China, political instability and turmoil aided the growth of Buddhism in Korea, whose rulers sought in Buddhism a protective force against constant foreign invasion. The underlying belief was that Buddhist deities, appeased by the erection of religious monuments and temples, would guarantee the well being of the country. During the Unified Silla period (668–935), a large number of temples were built in and around the capital Kyongju to ward off foreign armies, primarily the Chinese. Buddhism had both a powerful state and popular lay following throughout the Unified Silla period, as the Silla kings considered themselves to be incarnations of various Buddhas. The Koryo period (918–1392) commenced under Buddhist rule, and Buddhism continued to enjoy acceptance as Korea's artistic and educational focus, although by the twelfth century the religion began to lose its dominance in Korean culture. Buddhism lost its prominence at court when Confucianism became the official religion of the Choson dynasty (1392–1910), and, sadly, the vast majority of Buddhist monuments were destroyed. Buddhism has survived in Korean culture to the present by being assimilated into the older, native Korean folk traditions.

The original form of Buddhism that entered Korea was Mahayana as tempered by China, which stressed the role of bodhisattvas in attaining enlightenment and emphasized celestial realms, such as the Pure Land paradises of the Amitabha Buddha and bodhisattva Maitreya. A cult dedicated to the worship of Maitreya (Korean, Miroku) became popular by the end of the sixth century and increased during the Unified Silla period, when Silla kings considered themselves to be the personification of the bodhisattva.

The most distinctive of the early Korean Buddhist images is the seated, meditative bodhisattva with right leg crossed over the pendant left leg and the fingers of the right hand gently touching his cheek [cat. 44]. The pensive pose identifies the bodhisattva Maitreya seated in the Tushita Pure Land awaiting rebirth on earth as the Buddha of the future age. Many of these slender and elegant figures with youthful, smiling faces already displayed a unique Korean style by the sixth century, but very few images are known after the eighth century, indicating an eventual decline in the popularity of this cult. Of the many schools that entered Korea from China, Son (Chinese, Chan; Japanese, Zen), with its emphasis on meditation rather than scholasticism, was introduced in the seventh century and continues to characterize much of Buddhist practice in Korea today.

Buddhism finally reached Japan from the Korean kingdom of Paekche in either A.D. 538 or 552 with the presentation of Korean Buddhist images to the Japanese imperial court. The importance of Buddhism to Japan reached far beyond that of a new religious doctrine; Buddhism introduced a sophisticated Asian civilization to Japan in the form of literature, architecture, and the arts of painting and sculpture. At the same time, a new writing system and governmental structure were also imported to Japan from China and Korea. Initially, the arrival of Buddhism produced conflict between those of the ruling class who were willing to assimilate these new religious and aesthetic concepts into Japanese culture and those who felt it threatened both the native Shinto religion and the unquestioned authority of the emperor.

As was historically the case throughout Asia, Buddhism relied on imperial patronage for its early acceptance in Japan. The first great supporter of Buddhism was Prince Shotoku Taishi (574–622), who made it one of the state religions and commissioned the first Buddhist temples and monasteries. By the eighth century Buddhism had become emphatically linked to the imperial family by the founding of state temples (*kokubunji*) in the provinces that were under the leadership of the Todaiji temple in Nara, which was under imperial control. The great bronze image of the Buddha Vairocana in the Todaiji was symbolic of the sun, thus associating Buddhism with the sun divinities, the mythical founders of Japan. Imperial patronage was also instrumental in reconciling Buddhism with the native Shinto religion by allowing Shinto shrines to come under the protection of large Buddhist temples. In the tenth century the *suijaku* doctrine was developed, explaining that the Shinto deities (*kami*) were forms of Buddhist divinities. This doctrine was also expressed artistically, such as in sculptures of Hachiman, the popular Shinto god of war, depicted in the guise of a Buddhist monk [fig. 7].

The earliest Buddhist art in Japan dates from the beginning of the seventh century and took the form of votive bronze images. The Lotus Sutra and other Mahayana doctrines that emphasized the historical Buddha were first brought to Japan during the sixth century, and these early sculptures generally portrayed Shakyamuni. During the Asuka period (552–645), the Chinese Northern Wei style predominated, but some Buddhist sculpture was also influenced by Korean Paekche images of the meditating bodhisattva Maitreya [cat. 44]. The first real florescence of Buddhist art in Japan occurred in the Nara period (710–794). The dominant artistic influence came directly from contemporary Tang China and was evident in both Buddhist temple architecture and sculpture.

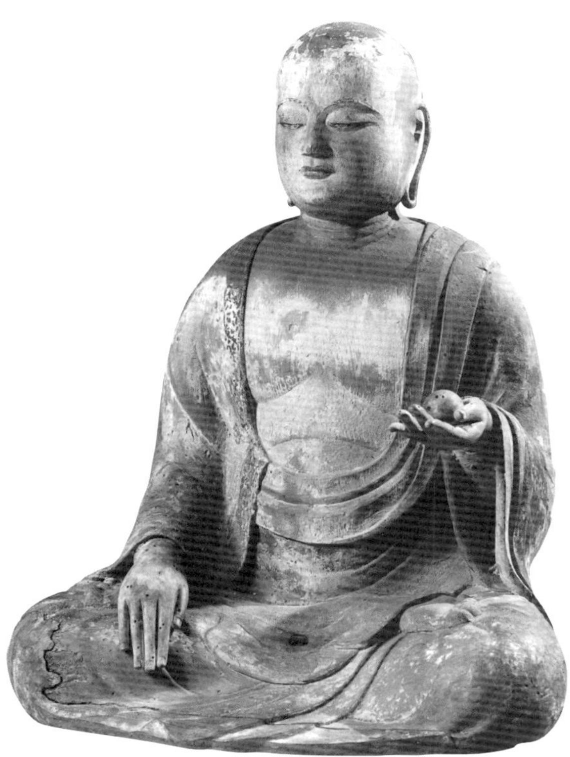

Hachiman in the Guise of a Buddhist Monk, Japan, Late Heian period, 11th century, polychromed wood, h. 19¼ in. (48.9 cm), Kimbell Art Museum, Fort Worth

At the beginning of the Heian period (794–1185) the capital moved from Nara to Kyoto and a more native Japanese style began to emerge. Buddhist art in the Early Heian period (794–897) was marked by the rise of esoteric schools and the ferocious deities associated with the esoteric Shingon sect. Shingon was introduced by the monk Kobo Daishi (774–835) in the ninth century and quickly gained popular appeal. Esoteric sects placed an emphasis on the entire pantheon of Buddhas and bodhisattvas, each having several manifestations. Buddhist sculpture of the Early Heian period was typified by the Jogan style, which was characterized by a certain archaism and rigidness of form; bodies were heavy, massive, and monolithic, and the facial expressions were often uninviting and lacking in the warmth normally associated with a compassionate being [cat. 49]. While esoteric Buddhism was favored from the ninth to the twelfth century, it was eventually eclipsed by the even more popular Pure Land schools.

Buddhism during the Late Heian period (897–1185), also called the Fujiwara period after the principal ruling family, was characterized by the marked increase in worship of the Amitabha Buddha's Western Pure Land, which became widespread during the following Kamakura period. This school of Buddhism taught that salvation could not be gained by performing good deeds or engaging in ritual meditation, but only through the mercy of Amitabha Buddha (Japanese,

Amida). Certain sects claimed that the ritual invocation of Amida's name "Namu Amida Butsu" (nembutsu) was sufficient to gain admittance to the Western Pure Land paradise. The increased interest in the Pure Land school resulted in a vast outpouring of works of art relating to Amida Buddha, and the courtly and more refined Fujiwara style endowed these images with an aura of purity and perfection. In Fujiwara-period sculptures of Amida, the drapery hugs the body and emphasizes soft contours; the silhouette is elongated with a slim torso and arms; and, above all, the face is possessed of an absolutely serene, meditative, and benevolent expression [cats. 50, 51]. The further assimilation of the Buddhist faith into the structure of Japanese society can be seen in the *raigo* doctrine of Pure Land Buddhism, especially popular from the eleventh to the thirteenth century, where the merciful Amida Buddha is imagined descending to a specific Japanese locality to guide the deceased practitioner to rebirth in the Western Pure Land. A whole class of art, both painted and sculpted, developed from this idea.

The Kamakura period (1185–1333) was noted for the emergence of military rulers. Subsequently, the genteel, courtly style of the eleventh and twelfth centuries gave way to the more dramatic and naturalistic traditions favored by the Kamakura military elite, inspiring an impressive body of muscular and violent sculpture in the late twelfth and thirteenth centuries. This military character was given particular expression in sculptures of the Four Guardian Kings (Japanese, Shi-Tenno; Sanskrit, Lokapala), protectors of the four corners of the world and the Buddhist Law, who were normally depicted in full armor. Their ferocious countenance and fierce poses, as they trample demons underfoot [cat. 53], were indicative of the intense realism and power of Kamakura-period sculpture.

Zen Buddhism (Chinese, Chan) was introduced during the Kamakura period and gained favor in the twelfth and thirteenth centuries. Zen was based on the Chinese Chan premise that the Buddha nature was inherent within each person and that meditation or concentration was the means to attaining self-realization. Zen dominated the arts of the ruling military class in the fourteenth and fifteenth centuries, and the Zen aesthetic continues to permeate the art and culture of Japan today, in the form of calligraphy, pottery, ink painting, garden design, flower arranging, and the tea ceremony.

After the fifteenth century, although Buddhism remained the principal religion of the Japanese populace, it no longer constituted a prime cultural force. Much of Buddhist art produced after the Kamakura period lost its vigor and creativity. The seventeenth-century Tokugawa regime (1615–1868) favored Confucianism, which brought about a decline in Buddhist practice; the production of large-scale sculpture decreased sharply, but smaller, portable, devotional images continued to be made. Because of the Japanese respect for the past, the great traditions of Japanese Buddhist art can still be seen today through the painstaking preservation of over 80,000 Buddhist temples and their contents.

•

By the fourth century B.C. India had established trade relations with the countries of Southeast Asia by way of sea routes that passed through ports in Sumatra, Java, and the Thai peninsula on the way to China. Along with goods came traders, missionaries, and Indian civilization. In addition to the Indian religious traditions of Hinduism and Buddhism, the Indian political concept of a government based on divine kingship was introduced, as well as the Sanskrit language and Indian alphabets. Throughout Southeast Asia, Hinduism and Buddhism were practiced side by side. In Cambodia and Vietnam (ancient Champa), Buddhism was not as important as Hinduism, with exceptions during certain periods when it enjoyed royal patronage. On the island of Java in Indonesia, Buddhism flourished in central Java in the eighth and ninth centuries but was ultimately assimilated into Hindu Shaivism. In Burma and Thailand, where Theravada Buddhism continues to be practiced, Buddhism experienced the most success.

It is not known when Hinduism was introduced, but the Indian emperor Ashoka Maurya was alleged to have sent Buddhist monks to Southeast Asia (probably Burma or Thailand) during the third century B.C. However, it was not until the second and third centuries A.D. that there was any significant association between India and Southeast Asia. The earliest surviving Buddhist images in Southeast Asia, dating from the fourth and fifth centuries A.D., were the bronzes brought from India and Sri Lanka by merchants and monks. The first locally made images date to the sixth century and demonstrate that regional styles were already developing. By this period a variety of Buddhist ethnic groups inhabited Thailand and Cambodia, each with a distinct culture and, in turn, a unique artistic style.

Mon sculptures may be the earliest indigenous sculptures in Southeast Asia. The Buddhist Mons migrated from Burma to Thailand sometime after the fifth century and controlled central Thailand and parts of Burma from the sixth through the tenth century. They adopted Theravada Buddhism and developed a distinctive Buddha image based on Indian prototypes of the Gupta-period Sarnath style, evident in the transparent, clingy robes that completely cover the body (giving little hint of the definition of musculature), the downcast eyes, snail-shell curls, and the *ushnisha*. However, Mon-style sculptures also reveal the physical traits of the local ethnic type. Mon Buddhas have square faces with high cheekbones, slanting eyes with arched eyebrows joined at the center, a broad nose and full lips, and display a rigid frontality as opposed to the more relaxed pose of Indian models.

The Khmers controlled Cambodia and parts of eastern Thailand from the sixth through the thirteenth century. Cambodian sculpture can be divided into two periods: the Pre-Angkor period, which lasted from the sixth to the ninth century, and the Angkor period, from the ninth to the fourteenth century. By the seventh century, Pre-Angkor sculptures from Cambodia and Vietnam already possessed many of the artistic qualities that distinguished Cambodian sculpture from Indian models: sculptures were carved in the round as opposed to high relief; they were not adorned with elaborate jewelry or clothing (rather, decoration was limited to hairstyles, miters, and the fashion in which their simple short garments were tied); and a greater sense of naturalism was achieved by highly polishing the stone, which brought the flesh to life. Pre-Angkor sculptures were well modeled with smooth-flowing transitions between body masses, and possessed of an aura of elegance as well as power, which provided the stylistic formula for Cambodian sculpture for the next three centuries [cat. 54].

Another regional style is represented by a group of bronzes unearthed in 1964 in the base of an abandoned temple in Prakhon Chai in Buriram province in northeast Thailand, which date from the seventh to the ninth century. Most of the sculptures represented the bodhisattva Maitreya, identified by the stupa in the hair [cat. 55], or the bodhisattva Avalokiteshvara, identified by the image of Buddha Amitabha in the hair [cat. 56], and a few were Buddhas. The bodhisattvas exhibit a combination of Mon and Khmer styles. Their minimal clothing and being cast in the round relate them to Pre-Angkor sculpture, while the lean and elegant proportions, relaxed pose, and introspective demeanor are more typical Mon characteristics.

In 802 King Jayavarman II laid the foundations for the Khmer empire, which would last until the fourteenth century and would unify Cambodia, parts of Thailand, and Vietnam. The Khmer capital was established at Angkor by the end of the ninth century; Angkor Wat was one of the greatest stone temples in the world. Beginning with Jayavarman II (r. 802–850), the Khmer kings were worshipped as incarnations of a deity, either Hindu or Buddhist, and thus ruled by divine right. The identification of a ruler

with a deity served to elevate the king to semidivine status, thus establishing the Cambodian concept of divine kingship, or god-king (*devaraja*). Sculptures of deities were both spiritual images as well as symbols of the ruler. Each Khmer king built a temple-mountain that served as a cosmic ritual center, a microcosm of the universe. The artistic style associated with each king was named after his temple-mountain. The variations in methods of wearing sampots and sarongs, wrapped skirts worn by males and females respectively, help to date different styles and probably reflected the changing fashions at court from one reign to the next. The classic Khmer style evolved by the tenth and eleventh centuries. Angkor-period sculptures show a remarkable continuity in face and body type, with an emphasis on massive forms and frontality. There is a marked contrast between the smooth, polished body surface and the finely detailed clothing, hairstyles, and crowns. By the tenth century, male deities were distinguished by the large powerful torsos, ample stomachs, wide hips, and heavy legs [cat. 58].

Jayavarman VII (r. 1181–1218) converted to Mahayana Buddhism and made it the state religion, thus becoming one of the greatest Cambodian patrons of Buddhist art. In so doing, he was breaking with precedent, as Hinduism had been the major religion of Khmer kings. Correspondingly, he ruled as a Buddha king rather than Hindu god-king and dedicated monuments to Buddhist rather than Hindu deities. The last and largest Khmer temple-mountain was the Bayon, built within the enormous Angkor Thom complex. Massive heads were incorporated into the stone architecture; the serenely smiling faces were carved in the physical likeness of the deified king.

A new type of Buddha image was emphasized during this period: a crowned Buddha seated on the coils of the serpent Muchalinda (*naga*), referring to the Buddha as a universal monarch [cat. 60]. The serpent represented the powers of water and was a symbol of royalty in Southeast Asia. This particular Buddha image became the focus of a cult, and Jayavarman VII may have had the Buddhas depicted in his own likeness. Carved stone "portraits" of Jayavarman VII embodied a combination of the physical human king and the metaphysical disposition of the Buddha [cat. 61]. These sublime qualities are seen in "portraits" of the queen as well [cat. 62].

Indian culture reached Indonesia by the fifth century A.D. As in mainland Southeast Asia, the earliest Buddhist images were imported Indian bronzes. The art of Indonesia shows greater stylistic affinities with the art of India, particularly the Pala style. From the seventh to the ninth century the kingdom of Shrivijaya, with its capital based in

Palembang, Sumatra, controlled parts of central and western Java and some of the Thai/Malay peninsula. By the late eighth and ninth centuries central Java had emerged as a prominent power in Southeast Asia. The Buddhism of the central Java period was largely influenced by Vajrayana (esoteric) concepts. The greatest confirmation of this was manifested in the construction of Borobudur in the ninth century, an enormous three-dimensional mandala, a cosmic diagram of the universe. The terraced stone structure, consisting of five rectangular and four circular levels, represents the journey from the earthly mundane plane of existence, to a world without desire, and finally to the apex, which represented the attainment of perfection. Over five hundred seated images of the Buddha cover the uppermost levels. Carved from local volcanic stone, the subtle modeling, wide faces, downcast eyes, and introspective gaze are a combination of Gupta and Pala styles [cat. 65].

Around 930 the Javanese court (*kraton*) inexplicably moved to eastern Java. The eastern Java period lasted until around 1520, when Islam became dominant. The esoteric practice of using mandalas continued through the creation of smaller, three-dimensional mandalas made of individual bronze figures. The Buddha Vairocana was normally the central deity of a mandala, with lower ranked deities, constituting his celestial family, surrounding and revering him [cat. 69]. Despite their diminutive size, these finely crafted bronzes are quite animated and display a profuse amount of detailed surface decoration. The extraordinary quality, variety, and abundance of these small bronze statues indicates the importance of three-dimensional mandalas during the eastern Java period.

The earliest evidence of Buddhism in Burma dates from the fifth century with the Mon settlements in lower Burma, but the political and cultural center of the Mon state was in central Thailand through the tenth century. Although Buddhism existed in Burma as early as it had in Thailand, the first appearance of a distinct Burmese style did not occur until the Pagan period (1044–1287). The Pala style was an early influence, but was soon transformed into a distinctive local style that would remain consistent. The Theravada,

Mahayana, and Vajrayana schools all coexisted at Pagan, but from the thirteenth century Theravada Buddhism became the dominant sect. The Theravada system cultivated the belief that merit could be gained each time an image of the Buddha was made. By the fourteenth century, the standard Burmese Buddha image was adorned with an elaborate crown and jewels and radiated an expression of serenity and benevolence [cat. 70].

During the thirteenth century as the Khmer empire weakened, the Thai people, who had migrated from south China and mixed with the existing Mon, formed a new Thai state. The first capital was established in 1240 at Sukhothai in north central Thailand and was consolidated in the mid-fourteenth century into the kingdom of Ayutthaya, named for the capital established in 1350 near present-day Bangkok. By the end of the fourteenth century a distinctive Thai school of Buddhist sculpture had emerged with the primary emphasis on Theravada Buddhism. The later sculpture of Thailand favored bronze over stone and is characterized by abstracted proportions and a striking geometrical stylization of forms [cat. 71].

Buddhist sculpture reaches across the boundaries of history and culture in its ability to convey to the viewer a universal concept of perfection, and therein lies its power. Although a fifteenth-century Thai Buddha is stylistically distant from the "classic" Indian Gupta Buddha of the fifth century, both images perfectly communicate the essence of spiritual transcendence and serve as a paradigm to all those who seek the path to enlightenment. The aesthetic triumph of Buddhist sculpture does not lie in the mastery of representing an external appearance of physical beauty, as in the classical traditions of the West, but rather in the ability to capture that which is intangible, an expression of absolute purity that radiates from within.

•

JENNIFER R. CASLER
Curator for Asian and Non-Western Art
Kimbell Art Museum, Fort Worth

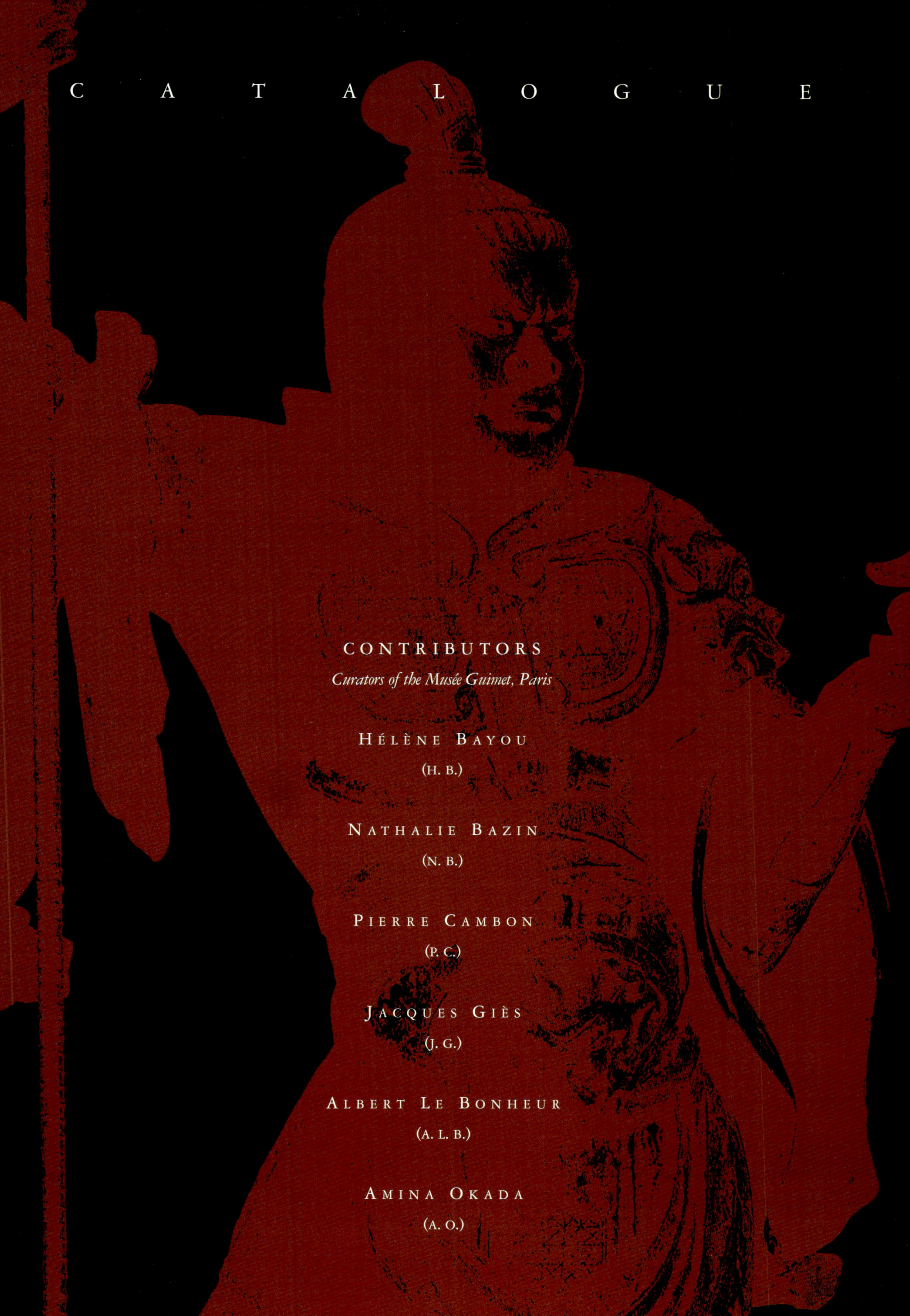

CATALOGUE

CONTRIBUTORS
Curators of the Musée Guimet, Paris

HÉLÈNE BAYOU
(H. B.)

NATHALIE BAZIN
(N. B.)

PIERRE CAMBON
(P. C.)

JACQUES GIÈS
(J. G.)

ALBERT LE BONHEUR
(A. L. B.)

AMINA OKADA
(A. O.)

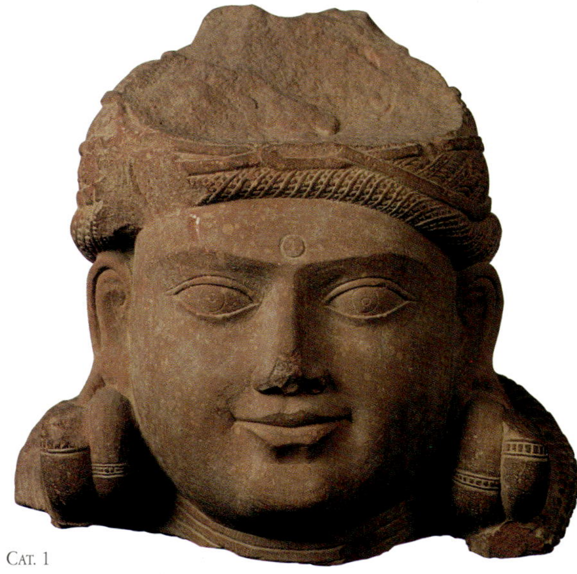

CAT. 1

1

Head of a Bodhisattva

India, Uttar Pradesh, Mathura region
Kushan period, second half of 1st–early 2nd century
Red sandstone; h. 17¾ in. (45 cm)
Musée Guimet, Paris MA 5935

Carved in red sandstone, this impressive head probably belonged to a heroically sized sculpture representing a bodhisattva. The turban, which in the monumental sculptures of the Kushan period distinguished a bodhisattva from a Buddha, was a constituent element of the Kushan nobility's dress. In the case of the bodhisattva images, it also evoked the secular life led by the Buddha before his enlightenment.

Now partially broken, the turban was originally topped by a large, rounded rosette; numerous sculptures in the round and reliefs from the Kushan period attest to its shape. Likewise, the "spiral" earrings frequently appear in Kushan art and are most often worn by bodhisattvas.

Though evidence of such imposing bodhisattva heads can certainly be found during the Kushan period, they are still scarce and resemble earlier prototypes. The Guimet sculpture, with its soothing and smiling aesthetics, at the same time polished and subtly archaic, could well date back to the second half of the first century or the beginning of the second century.

A. O.

2

Nagaraja

India, Uttar Pradesh, Mathura region
Kushan period, 2nd century
Red sandstone; h. 45⅞ in. (116 cm)
Musée Guimet, Paris MG 18214

Generally appearing in a semi-anthropomorphic form, the *naga* are serpent kings associated with water. They serve as protective spirits, keepers of the treasures hidden within the bowels of the earth, and they are said to inhabit the Patala, one of seven subterranean regions, and to reside in marvelous palaces studded with precious gems. Helpful and benevolent, they became part of the Buddhist pantheon and were worshipped by the agricultural class because of their power to cause fertilizing rainfalls, guaranteeing rich crops

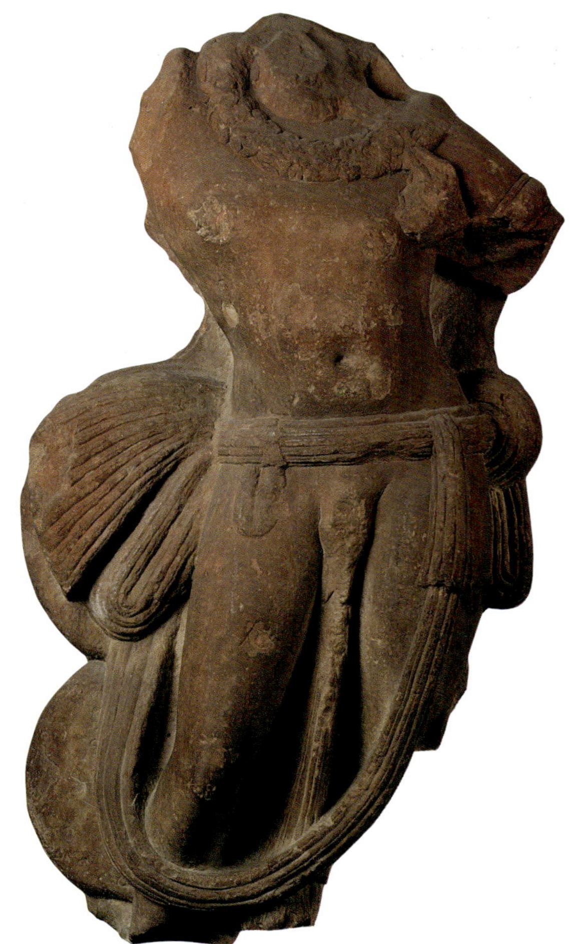

CAT. 2

and ensuring prosperity. Their effigies were often placed outside, close to cisterns and reservoirs, which they were able to fill up due to their particular powers.

The *Nagaraja*'s hips are covered with a diaphanous *dhoti* held in place by a wide cloth belt that majestically drapes down toward the knees and forms a large loop; a flower garland adorns his neck. The representation of the garb and especially the belt, whose folds are evoked by deep incisions, as well as the vigorous and naturalistic modeling of the body, with its robust but harmonious forms, are characteristic of the Kushan art of Mathura.

A. O.

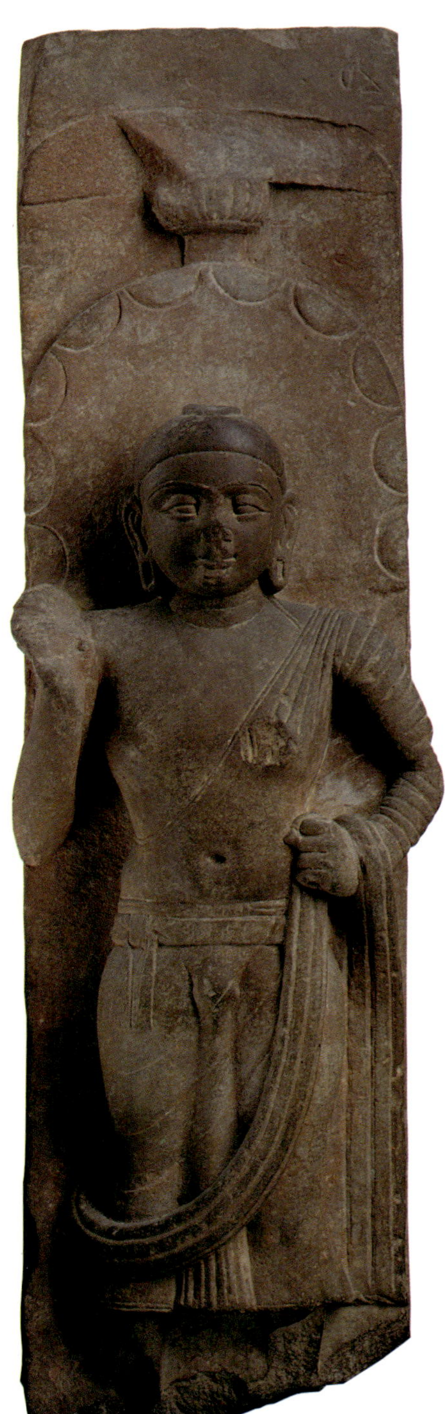

3

Stupa Post with Buddha

India, Uttar Pradesh, Mathura region
Kushan period, end of 1st–early 2nd century
Red sandstone; h. 27½ in. (70 cm)
Musée Guimet, Paris MG 17849

Carved in very high relief on the post of a stupa balustrade, the Buddha is depicted in a standing position, wearing a monastic robe that leaves the right shoulder bare. His right hand is raised at shoulder height with the open palm facing outward in the gesture of reassurance (*abhaya-mudra*). His left hand holds a panel of the monastic robe, which falls in folds gathered on the left side. The head is outlined by a halo whose edges are decorated by small arches and is topped by a sunshade, a symbol of royalty. The *urna*, one of the signs of the Buddha's preeminence (*lakshana*), is visible at the junction of the eyebrows, although here the cranial protuberance (*ushnisha*) is evoked only by the particular shape of the partly broken *kaparda*, the twisted bun.

In the art of ancient India, *kapardin*-type Buddhas are the first images in human form of the Buddha, who, until then, had been depicted only through explicit symbols. The sculpture, with its strong relief, is characteristic of the first- and second-century Kushan style, which is dominated by robust and massive forms, coarse features, and smiling faces with slightly bulging eyes that are accented by the double curving lines of the eyebrows. The ample curve of the cloth of the monastic garment is another feature typical of the Kushan art of Mathura, as is the large scalloped halo, which is inseparable from the sculptural vocabulary of the *kapardin*-type Buddha.

A. O.

29

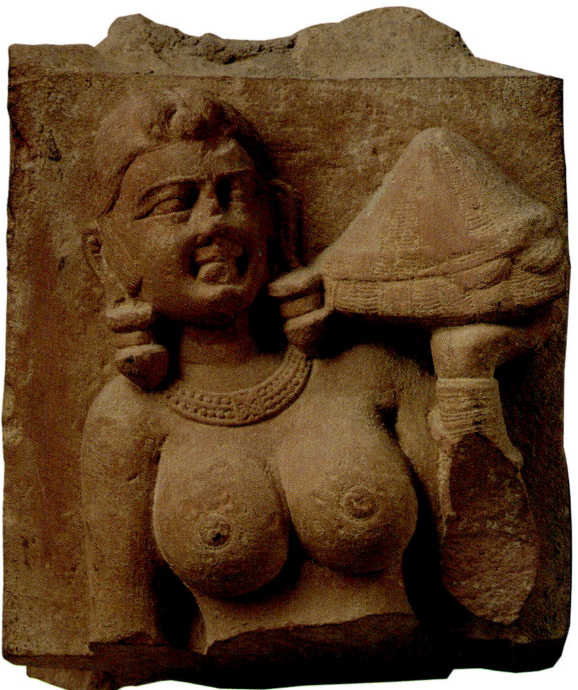

abundance. The right hand, now broken, may have held an ewer filled with holy water destined to consecrate the gift. The woman's features—slightly bulging eyes, well-defined corners of the mouth, elaborate hairdo, and detailed ornaments, notably the "top"-shaped earrings—are characteristic of the period.

A. O.

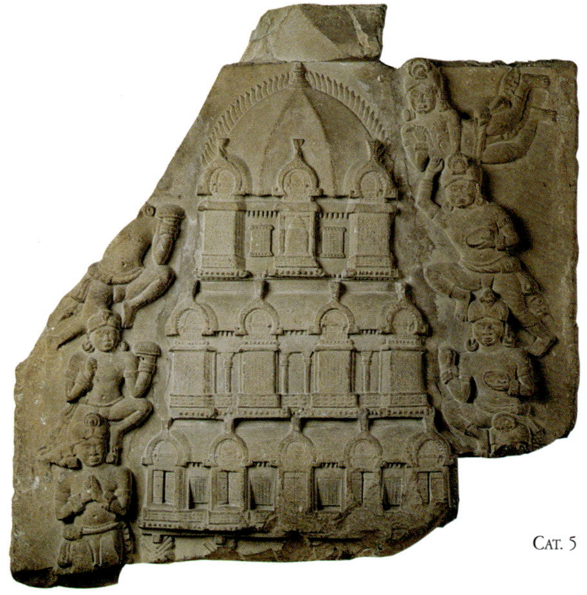

4

Fragment of a Balustrade with a Woman Carrying an Offering

India, Uttar Pradesh, Mathura region
Kushan period, mid–2nd century
Red sandstone; h. 16⅞ in. (43 cm)
Musée Guimet, Paris MA 4798

Balustrades were used to protect the sacred enclosure of a sanctuary or a stupa. In the Kushan period, balustrade posts were decorated on the exterior side with divine and beneficial motifs, offering a gracious anthology of full-shaped and sensual feminine deities who evoked the immemorial themes of abundance and fertility. These nymphs and dryads, associated with trees, could by their mere presence or the subtle touch of their hand cause the branches to bloom. Since the representation of female beauty was a source of blessing, the devout could benefit just by looking at these minor deities. They are usually surrounded by women carrying offerings, whose images are also beneficial since they glorify the gesture of giving, which allows the devout to become more worthy.

It is the image of such a woman carrying an offering that graces the Guimet balustrade post. The woman carries a woven basket in her left hand at shoulder height. The lid has slipped, allowing the garlands to spill out—a symbol of

5

Relief with Tiered Sanctuary

India, Andhra Pradesh, Ghantasala
Amaravati school, end of 1st–early 2nd century
Marmoreal limestone; h. 45⅝ in. (116 cm)
Musée Guimet, Paris MG 17851

The central part of this relief is taken up by a religious edifice whose architecture is elaborate; its identification remains uncertain. The work presents itself as a tiered tower with a circular plan and exposed framework; the three floors are topped by an octagonal dome. The upper floor has a balcony sheltering a stupa-shrine; the halo of flames radiating from the edifice's dome expresses the sacred nature of the relic enshrined within the reliquary. A horseshoe-shaped arch (called *gavaksa*, bull's-eye), decorated with exposed beams—a motif frequently used by Indian architects to decorate temples and sanctuaries—tops the balconied windows of the building, evoking the wooden frames of the ancient constructions.

Two donors or worshippers, their hands joined in a gesture of tribute (*anjali*), appear on each side of the shrine; only the turban now remains from the worshipper on the right. Six flying genies are loaded with various offerings—flower garlands and cups that may be full of butter balls or flower petals—which they seem to be throwing on the shrine by the handful as a sign of piety.

This stupa cover panel may well date back to the end of the first century or the second century A.D.; the relatively naive treatment of the figures, with their awkward proportions and clumsy postures, indicates a certain archaism.

A. O.

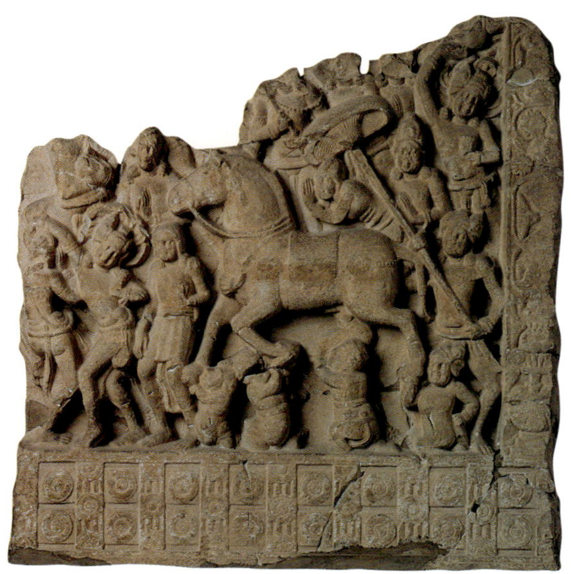

CAT. 6

6

Relief with "The Great Departure"
India, Andhra Pradesh, Amaravati region
Amaravati school, 2nd century
Marmoreal limestone; h. 35⅜ in. (90 cm)
Musée Guimet, Paris MG 18509

This relief illustrates Prince Siddhartha's "Great Departure," when, at nightfall, he secretly flees the Kapilavastu royal palace and secular life in search of the truth. The scene is dominated by the central presence of Kanthaka, Prince Siddhartha's horse, harnessed but without a rider. In order to suggest the virtual presence of the prince

mounting his horse, a figure carrying a sunshade, symbol of royalty, appears on the right; a servant carrying a fly whisk (the head is broken) and two worshippers, hands together in the gesture of tribute (*anjali*), are depicted in the upper part. In front of the horse walks Chandaka, the prince's squire, wearing the short pleated tunic characteristic of his status. The numerous persons animating the scene include two serpent kings (*nagaraja*) and four genies, or *yakshas*, keepers of the gates and cities, who support Kanthaka's hooves with their hands to smother the noise of the horse's gallop and protect Prince Siddhartha's flight.

The style of this relief, marked by its dense but clever composition and an impression of continuous movement, illustrates the blossoming phase of Amaravati art found in the second and early third centuries, when the figures become more refined and animated. Stupa cover panels illustrating Prince Siddhartha's flight are generally represented with the horse in profile and going toward the left so that the faithful, who according to custom always walked around a sacred edifice in the direction of the sun while keeping the monument on their right side, could perceive the chronological unfolding of the illustrated episodes.

A. O.

7

Relief with the Conversion and Ordination of Nanda and Battle Scene (The War of the Relics?)
India, Andhra Pradesh, Nagarjunakonda
Amaravati school, 3rd century
Marmoreal limestone; h. 28⅜ in. (72 cm)
Musée Guimet, Paris MG 17069

This stupa cover panel consists of two illuminated registers separated by an ornamental frieze. The upper register illustrates the edifying story of Prince Nanda, the Buddha's half-brother, who, in spite of his unwillingness, was converted and ordained a Buddhist monk. The left side of the relief shows Nanda still dressed and outfitted as a prince, standing under a *torana*. His head, without the princely turban, reveals his newly cropped hair.

The right side of the relief shows the Buddha seated on a throne placed under the bodhi tree, wearing a monastic robe and making the gesture of blessing (*varadamudra*) with his right hand. A servant behind the throne, carrying a fly whisk, may represent the bodhisattva Vajrapani, Buddha's

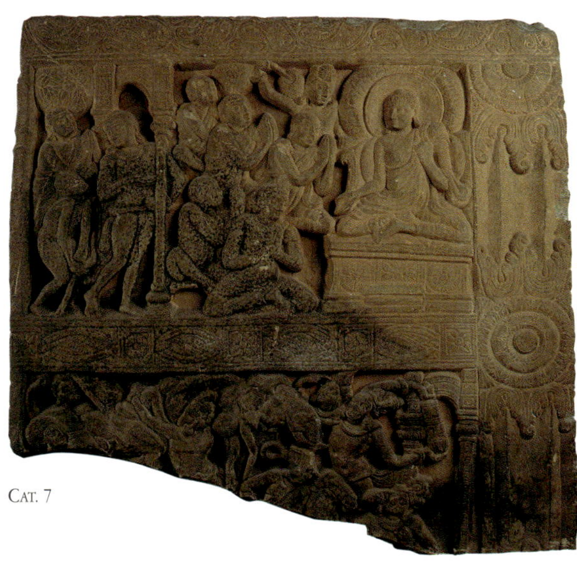

left post of the *torana*, which outlines the figure in low relief. The Buddha appears to have been making the gesture of reassurance (*abhayamudra*), with the hand raised at shoulder height, palm facing forward. The Buddha's face, with its somewhat bulging eyes and heavy eyelids, has slightly elongated features lit by a subtle smile. He bears the preeminence marks (*lakshana*) characteristic of exceptional beings—the *urna* between the eyebrows and the *ushnisha*, a cranial protuberance covered with flat curls ritually coiled towards the right—and stands out against a smooth halo.

This Buddha is a perfect example of Amaravati images from the end of the second and the beginning of the third century, which slowly evolved into a genre that became more popular with the passing centuries in Ceylon and even in areas of Southeast Asia. The treatment of the heavy monastic robe draped in the manner of a Roman toga may be a consequence of the flourishing trade existing between south India and the Roman world during the first centuries A.D.

A. O.

faithful companion. Five monks are seated at the feet of the Buddha, hands joined in the *anjali* gesture; the monk seated in the first row may very well be Nanda.

The lower register, largely incomplete, shows a lively and animated battle that may evoke the War of the Relics, when the chiefs of seven clans faithful to the Buddha opposed the king of the Malla, who had stolen the Buddha's holy relics.

This panel is distinguished by its low relief carving, the coarse and stereotyped features of the figures, and its clever and balanced composition. The floral and plant motifs framing the illuminated registers resemble the decoration of numerous reliefs also excavated at Nagarjunakonda, the Buddhist site where the Amaravati school flourished in the third and fourth centuries.

A. O.

8

Standing Buddha

India, Andhra Pradesh, Ghantasala?
Amaravati school; late 2nd–early 3rd century
Marmoreal limestone; h. 29⅞ in. (76 cm)
Musée Guimet, Paris MG 17850

Depicted in a frontal position, in high relief, this *Standing Buddha* wears a heavy monastic robe draped in large, regular folds, which leaves the right shoulder bare; the left arm clutches the tail end against the chest. The right hand has been broken but a trace of it remains visible on the

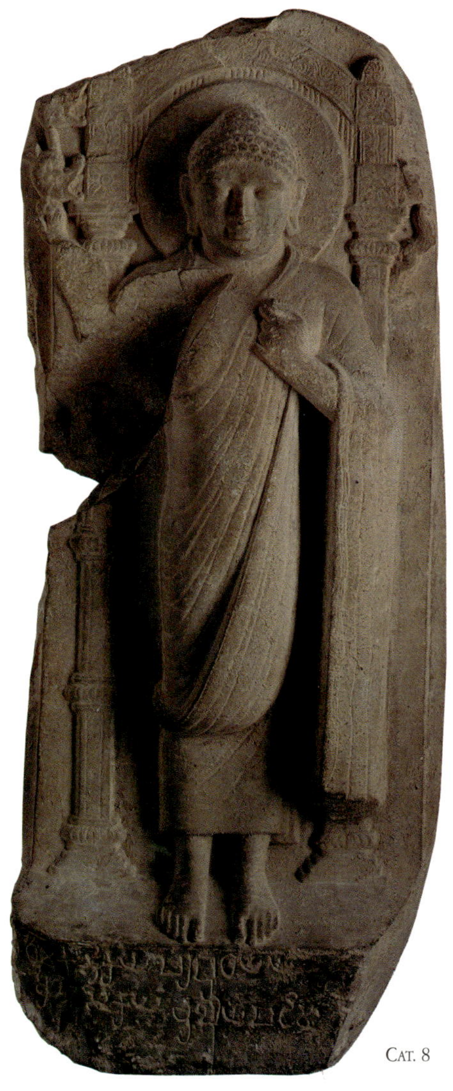

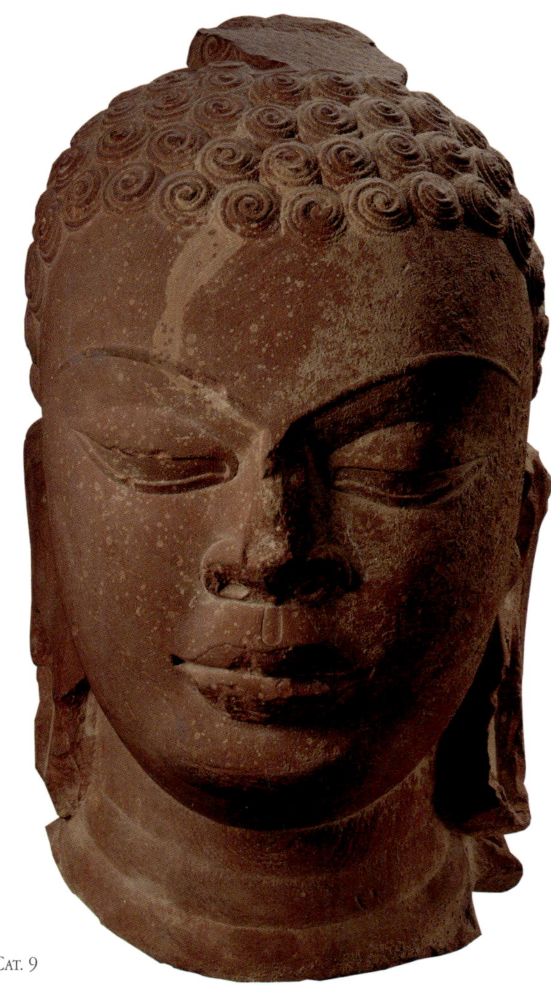

9

Head of Buddha

India, Uttar Pradesh, Mathura
Gupta period, c. 430–435
Pink sandstone; h. 19⅝ in. (50 cm)
Musée Guimet, Paris MA 5029

The Buddhas of the Gupta period figure among the most perfect expressions of Indian Buddhist art. This *Head of Buddha* illustrates the smiling serenity and proud beauty of these works, where the nobility of the Buddhist ideal subtly harmonizes with the refined criteria of an art that has reached its peak.

Carved in pink sandstone, the work is distinguished by its extremely fine execution, noticeable, in particular, in the streamlined facial features and smooth modeling. The cranial protuberance (*ushnisha*), one of the thirty-two marks of preeminence of exceptional beings (*lakshana*), is covered, as is the skull, by locks of hair that are ritually coiled toward

the right. Of the eighty additional marks, this Buddha head possesses the eyebrows, doubly curving inward like the bow of an archer, and a neck that resembles the upper part of a conch and is marked by parallel folds, a stylistic element systematized in the Gupta period.

Of special interest are the lined eyes with heavy lowered eyelids, bestowing a meditative expression to the face, which is filled with inwardness and detachment as well as a certain abstraction. This feature—the half-closed eyes lowered toward the faithful, as if to invite them to meditate—seems to have appeared in Mathura around 390–395; it subsequently became characteristic of Buddhist and Jain images, setting them apart from the earlier works of the Kushan period, where the eyes are wide open, seemingly staring at the faithful. Considering its imposing dimensions, the Guimet's *Head of Buddha* may have belonged to a seated Buddha (approximately sixty inches high) rather than to a standing figure.

A. O.

10

Buddha

India, Uttar Pradesh, Mathura
Gupta period, first half or mid-5th century
Pink sandstone; h. 55⅞ in. (142 cm)
Musée Guimet, Paris MA 4864

Depicted frontally and in a standing position, this Buddha of the Mathura school exhibits a fluid and elongated shape, subtle modeling, and precise execution. His head, which unfortunately has disappeared, stood out against a large, circular halo. The right hand, also broken, was probably stretched out palm forward in the gesture of reassurance (*abhayamudra*); the left hand clutches the tail of the monastic robe, whose regular, concentric, U-shaped folds reveal a slender body. The undergarment held at the waist by a knotted cord can also be made out underneath the transparent monastic robe. The transparent effect of the robe may have been an endeavor to translate into stone one of the thirty-two preeminence marks (*lakshana*) of the Buddha, suggesting the golden glow of the body of the Buddha, who, following the enlightenment, has started to shine with a heavenly light.

Only a fragment of the circular halo, which is characteristic of the Gupta style, remains. Its abundant decoration, placed in concentric sections, consists of lotus petals, a radiate floral motif; foliated scrolls (among which one can

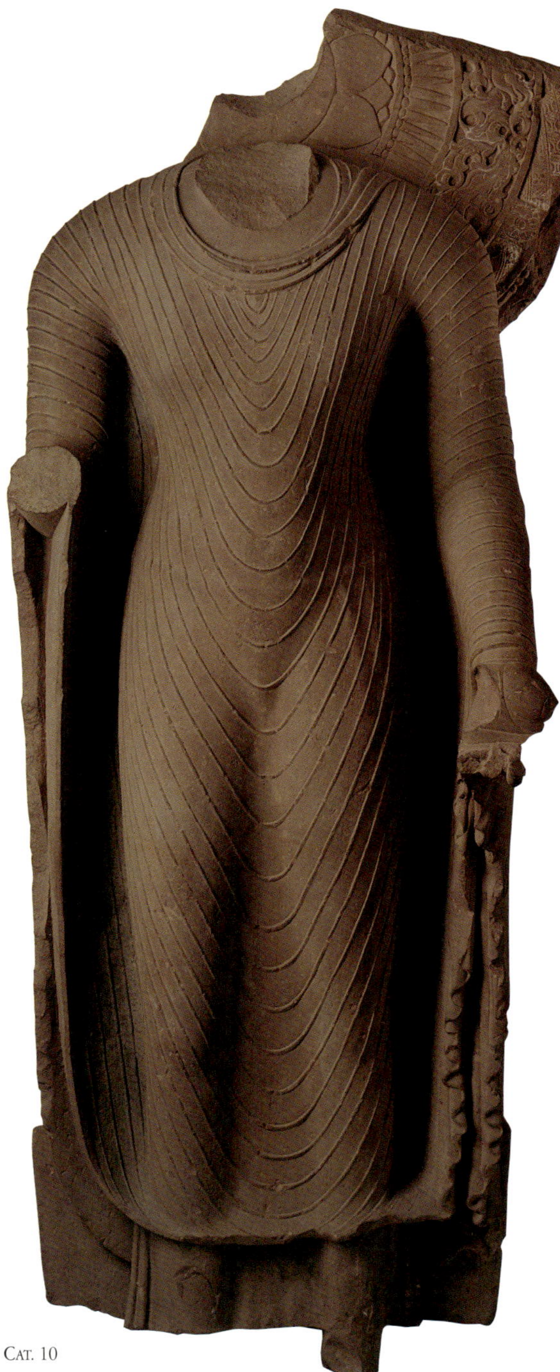

barely note the presence of a bird holding a cluster of grapes
[?] in its beak, an ancient motif for a good omen); and a coil
of decorated braids. The polychromatic traces remaining on
the halos of other surviving Gupta Buddha heads indicate
that the pieces were originally enhanced through coloring.

A. O.

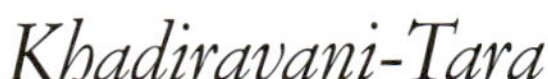

11

Khadiravani-Tara

India, Bihar; Pala period, 9th century
Gray sandstone; h. 23⅜ in. (60 cm)
Musée Guimet, Paris MA 2480

This stele represents the goddess Tara appearing as
Khadiravani-Tara ("Tara of the acacia woods," on Mount
Potala), surrounded by her usual assistants, Marici and
Ekajata. The female counterpart of bodhisattva Avalokiteshvara, and, like him, a savior of creatures in danger, Tara
is one of the protective and sympathetic deities whose cult
was developed in India and Tibet. Standing on a lotus, her
hips slightly swaying and covered with jewels, the goddess
makes the gesture for charity (*varadamudra*) with her right
hand and holds in her now broken left hand her distinctive
attribute, the blue lotus. Her head, graced by a tiara, stands
outlined against a large halo edged by a pearly coil bordered
with stylized flames, in which is inscribed the Buddhist
creed. Behind the goddess the high back of a seat is decorated with rearing lions.

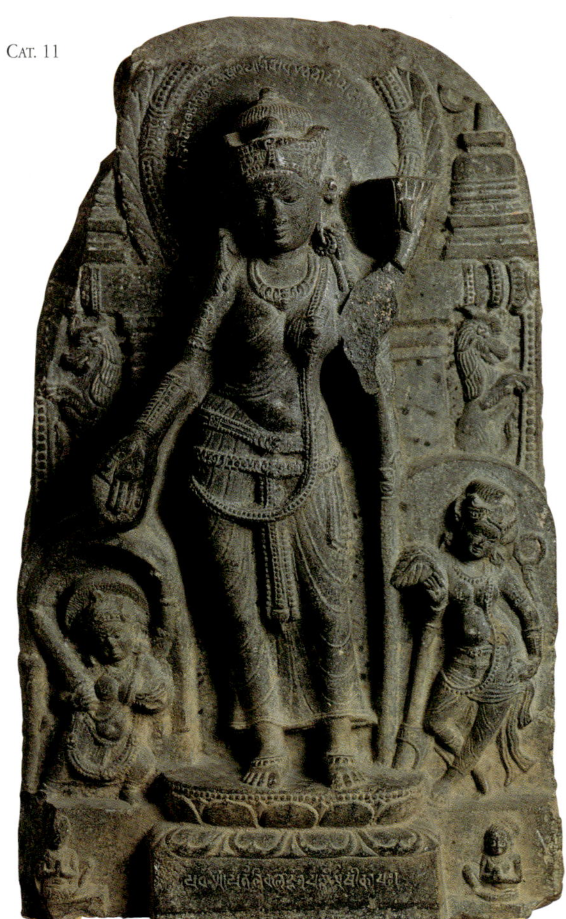

Ekajata is at the left, carrying in her lower hands the sword and skullcap and in her upper hands, raised above her head, the elephant carcass. To the right, Marici, her right arm leaning on an ax, holds in both hands the *asoka* branch and the lace. Two donors, hands joined in the *anjali* gesture, appear on the pedestal.

The soft modeling full of curves, the rendering of the clothes and ornaments, and even the decoration of the halo's edge allow us to trace this work back to the Bihar artistic production of the ninth century.

A. O.

12

Relief with "The Great Departure"
Pakistan, Gandhara; Kushan period, 1st–3rd century
Schist; 10⅛ x 23⅜ in. (27.1 x 59.3 cm)
Musée Guimet, Paris MG 17052

It is in Gandhara that for the first time deliberately "pedagogical" works appear that tell the story of the historical Buddha. This relief in gray schist is typical of Gandharan art, a hybrid style that developed in the northwest of India during the reign of the great Kushans and their successors. It evokes the episode when Siddhartha is suddenly aware of the emptiness of his existence in his father's palace and decides to break away from his life as a prince. Here, the scene is told in an abbreviated form, since only Siddhartha's spouse, Yasodhara, is depicted asleep on the couch. The bodhisattva appears to have just decided to leave the palace, never to come back, and is seated very straight on the edge of the realistically rendered bed, raising his hand to communicate his absence of fear. His faithful squire, Chandaka, comes in from the left, carrying a turban and bringing the prince's favorite steed, Kanthaka.

In this slightly inward curving panel, the sculptor somewhat clumsily and naively plays on attitudes and per-

spectives to animate the scene. To the right, a woman of imposing size stands guard, armed with a lance, perhaps one of the foreigners who were said to be Greek and constituted some of the favorite entourage of the Indian rulers. At the top, a balcony between two arcades, supported by pillars of a vaguely Corinthian style, symbolizes the palace, with figures subtly cut out behind the balustrade. The central figure appears to have wings and raises his hand in a gesture of appeasement.

P. C.

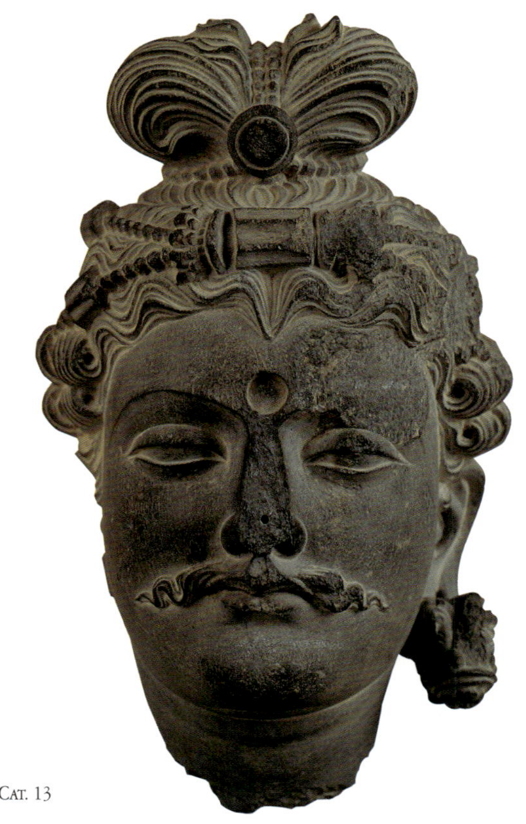

Cat. 13

13

Head of a Bodhisattva
Pakistan, Gandhara, Buner
Kushan period, 1st–3rd century
Schist; h. 12¾ in. (32.5 cm)
Musée Guimet, Paris AO 2911

This bodhisattva head was brought back by Alfred Foucher from his excavations in Gandhara, on the Afghan border, in 1895–97. The nose is straight, the eyes well-defined, the face a smooth oval adorned by an elegantly upturned mustache—as was the fashion in the northwest of

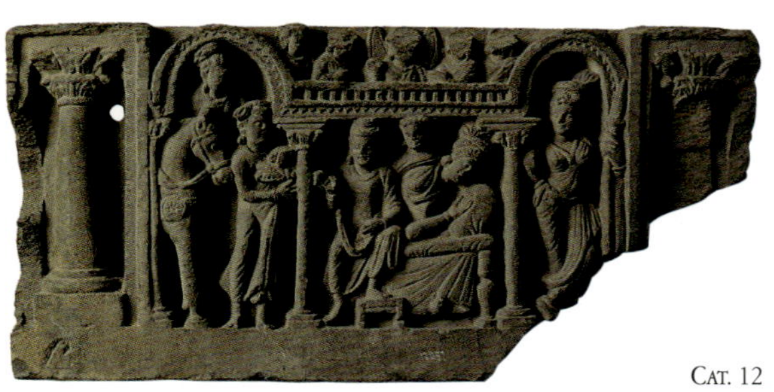

Cat. 12

35

India, where Buddhist art at the time of the great Kushans was impregnated with Hellenistic traditions.

With the *urna* between the eyes, the ears weighed down by jewels in the Indian fashion, and with a rare motif showing three lions, this face suggests a clearly secular person, which has led some scholars to suggest that Gandharan bodhisattvas—of which there are numerous and diverse surviving examples—sometimes represented local rulers. This impression is strengthened by the naturally wavy hair brought up in a bun on top of the head and held together by a voluminous jewel, with a string of pearls holding a rectangular-shaped cabochon on the forehead.

While Foucher recognized a Greco-Buddhist style in the art of this border region, the image appears to be clearly "Indian"; the occidental influences, with their Hellenistic type of realism, are here integrated in a new art form whose effeminate grace and somewhat languid charm echoes traditions that originated in the north or even in Iran.

P. C.

14

Standing Bodhisattva
Pakistan, Gandhara, Shahbaz-Garhi
Kushan period, 1st–3rd century
Schist; h. 47¼ in. (120 cm)
Musée Guimet, Paris AO 2907

This bodhisattva is one of the most famous of the one hundred pieces brought back by Foucher in 1895–97 from his excavations in the northwest of India, on the Afghan border, and was exhibited in the Louvre as early as 1900. Standing proudly, one hand on his hip, the other making the gesture indicating absence of fear, the statue is typical of the hybrid art from Gandhara, which Foucher described as "Greco-Buddhist." This prince, with his purely Apollonian profile, is dressed like an Indian ruler, wearing the *dhoti*, bare-chested, with a sash casually slung over his shoulder and draped in an elegant curve over the forearm. The haloed figure has a mustache, and his turban is topped with a tuft of feathers that appears strange in the Buddhist context.

This bodhisattva's eclectic ensemble mixes Indian influences with Scythian gold jewelry featuring definite Greco-Roman elements, such as the necklace decorated with putti, straight from the Mediterranean, or the two little angels on either side of the medallion decorating his hairdo.

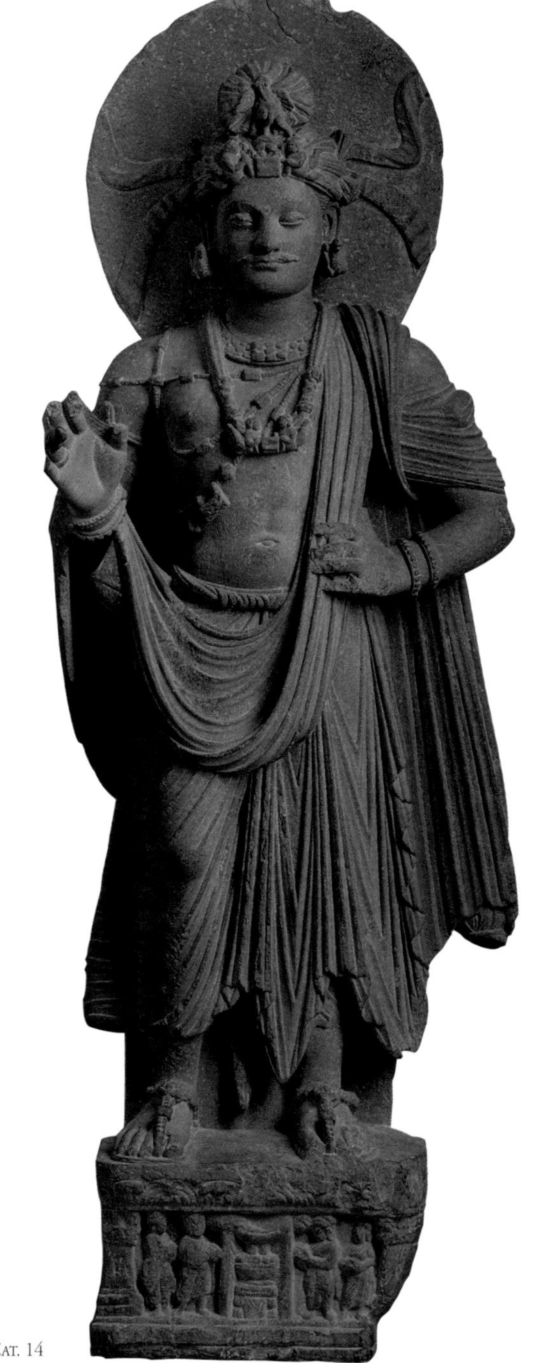

CAT. 14

If the sandals are Greek and have a lion mask on top of each foot, the Indian-type earrings, however, borrow from the Iranian fashion. The figure shows the *urna* between the eyes; the fingers of his right hand are maintained by a palmed membrane revealing his superhuman nature, according to the canonical texts of the Buddhist religion. Finally, the pedestal itself is decorated in an explicit manner with a scene from the Buddhist tradition, the adoration of Buddha's alms bowl by visibly secular donors.

P. C.

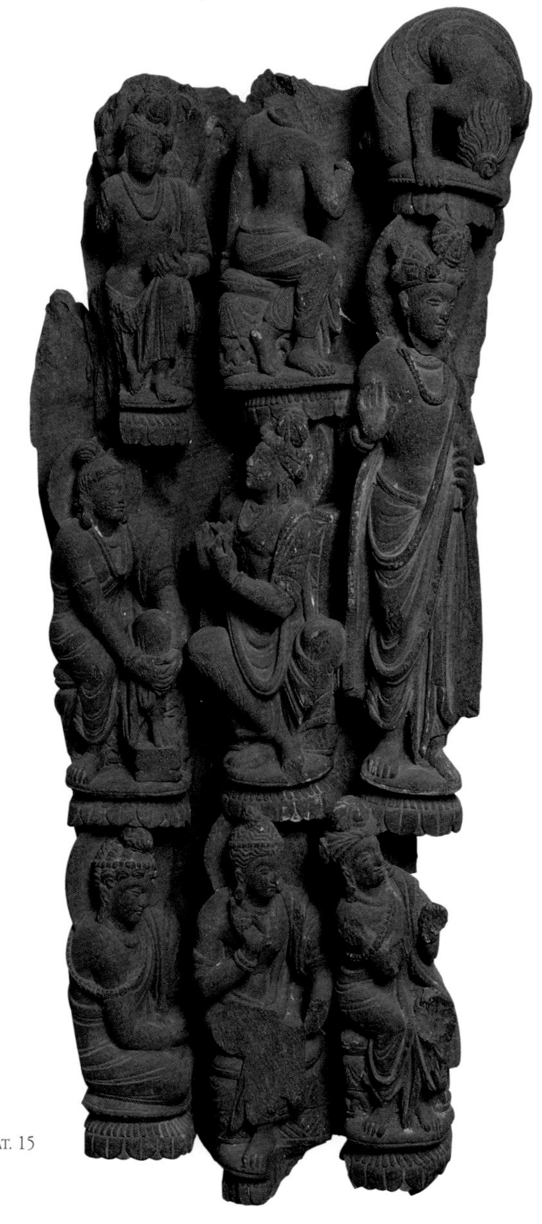

sketches. The artist realizes an amazingly complex composition, but at the same time renders a perfectly natural group—lively, charming, and extremely harmonious—and plays on the interplay of looks and attitudes between the figures. At the top, the figure holding a book leans forward as if better to listen, his neighbor turns away and is shown from the back, and the third figure is bending over, his head touching the ground. At the bottom, a figure meditates, apparently lost in his inner dream, the second figure listens attentively and seriously, his hand cupped close to his ear, and the third figure backs up a little and lifts his head, as if delighted by what he seems to see and hear. The middle tier holds two figures who are deeply engulfed in conversation, visibly uninterested in their surroundings.

The whole scene is dominated by the imposing figure wearing a turban, who holds a lotus in one hand, the other making the gesture expressing absence of fear. The lotus carrier can be identified as Padmapani (or Avalokiteshvara), symbolizing Buddhist compassion. The virtuosity of the sculptor is evident in the manner in which he plays with relief and volumes and in his success in creating a deliberately dynamic perspective that very cleverly uses shadows or light. This artist shows an inventiveness, a real imagination, and a new sense of composition. In this work, Gandharan sculpture has definitely freed itself from the stone, showing the profound evolution and the distance covered since the very first purely narrative reliefs came out of this school during the era of the great Kushans.

P. C.

15

Buddhist Gathering

Pakistan, Gandhara, Mardan region
Kushan period, 1st–3rd century
Schist; h. 26⅜ in. (67 cm)
Musée Guimet, Paris MA 3757

This fragment of a stele in very high relief, almost like a sculpture in the round, depicts a Buddhist gathering that probably took place around a figure (now lost), a Buddha who was most likely seated on a lotus whose stem plunged in the middle of a pond. Placed on three tiers, these small figures, surprisingly animated, are portrayed as if individual

16

Bodhisattva

Pakistan, Gandhara; Kushan period, 3rd–4th century
Schist; h. 17¾ in. (45 cm)
Musée Guimet, Paris MG 18915

With its smile and sweet face, this bust of a genie or bodhisattva, his head slightly bent, evokes the Gothic angels of the Reims style. The free-flowing locks, held by a classical-style torus, tumble in natural curls over the forehead and down the shoulders of this very young prince. Bare-chested, a coat draped over his shoulder, he wears the Brahmanic cord across his chest and a large, flat piece of Scythian-style gold jewelry around his neck. Aside from his shoulder necklace and his richly decorated bracelets, he also wears a chain and pendant whose motif could frequently be

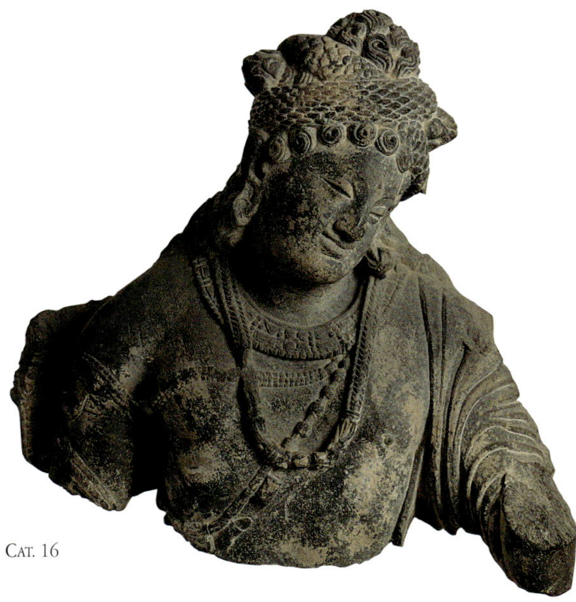

CAT. 16

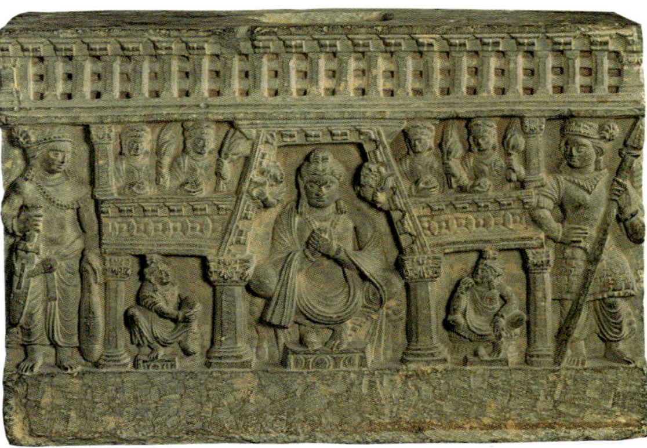

CAT. 17

found on Gandharan soil: the heads of two deer facing each other. With his adolescent charm, this almost feminine bodhisattva was very likely part of a triad or maybe even a group with the figure of the Buddha at its center. His slightly oblique position illustrates the compassion of these mediators—typical of Buddhism—who became more frequent as the figure of Shakyamuni became more and more abstract, theoretical, and remote. Through the harmonious balance of composition and proportions, this bodhisattva appears to be one of the truly successful pieces of Gandharan art.

P. C.

17

Relief with the Bodhisattva Maitreya in Tushita Heaven

Afghanistan, Gandhara, Shotorak Monastery
Kushan period, 3rd–5th century
Schist; 11¾ x 17¼ in. (29.7 x 43.8 cm)
Musée Guimet, Paris MG 18962

A bodhisattva sits on a throne supported by two columns topped with remotely Corinthian capitals, his legs crossed, hands held in a single *mudra*, with the left hand turned towards the chest, partly hiding the fingers of the right hand. On each side, two ridiculously small assistants, dressed like princes and wearing turbans, listen to him with sustained attention. They both look very natural, depicted in relaxed, almost nonchalant poses, contrasting with the immobility of the huge and majestic central figure, frozen in

its eternal and silent preaching. In the balconies on each side, two women, shown only from the waist up, are turning toward the bodhisattva as if to render homage, holding a fruit in one hand and a palm frond in the other. Watching on either side are two gigantic guards, conferring a barbaric dignity, a military harshness, solemn and savage, to the scene. These are the famous Yavana mentioned in the Indian texts, the foreigners frequently recruited by the local rulers to serve as palace guards.

This is a perfectly defined composition, appearing curiously static, a mixture of abstraction and naturalism, realistic attitudes and frontality. The relief, though typical of Gandharan art, also has a rather hieratic, almost monumental style, influenced by the Parthian and Iranian fashion. On this low relief, Maitreya is enthroned in Tushita Heaven, the heaven of thirty-three gods, before descending to earth as a future Buddha. His appearance as an Indian prince—the scarf draped over his shoulders, the necklaces, the earrings—points, as does his size, toward his role as mediator and bodhisattva. The hair in a bun evokes Maitreya, as does the attitude—seated with legs crossed—in which he is often depicted in Gandhara as well as in Central Asia.

P. C.

18

Buddha with Great Miracle

Afghanistan, Gandhara, Paitava
Kushan period, Kapica school, 3rd–4th century
Schist, traces of gilding; h. 31⅞ in. (81 cm)
Musée Guimet, Paris MG 17478

Unearthed during the 1924 Joseph Hackin excavations at the site of the Paitava Buddhist foundation, this *Buddha with Great Miracle* is undoubtedly from the Kushan era. The stele "realistically" describes one of the episodes of the Great Miracle of Sravasti, where the Buddha demonstrates his power to the assembly of heretical masters. The lotus of the Law is engraved in the palm of the right hand. Indra and Brahma, the gods of Hinduism, humbly hold the sunshade above Buddha's head to express their respect. This high relief demonstrates the typical style of the border region of the Iranian plateau and Central Asia. It moves away from the classical Gandharan model by virtue of its clearly affirmed frontality, the massive aspect of the image, and the disproportion between the figures and the donors kneeling below; the emphasis has been placed on the monumental character of the Buddha, who is represented standing, with flames coming out of his shoulders and water flowing out of his feet.

P. C.

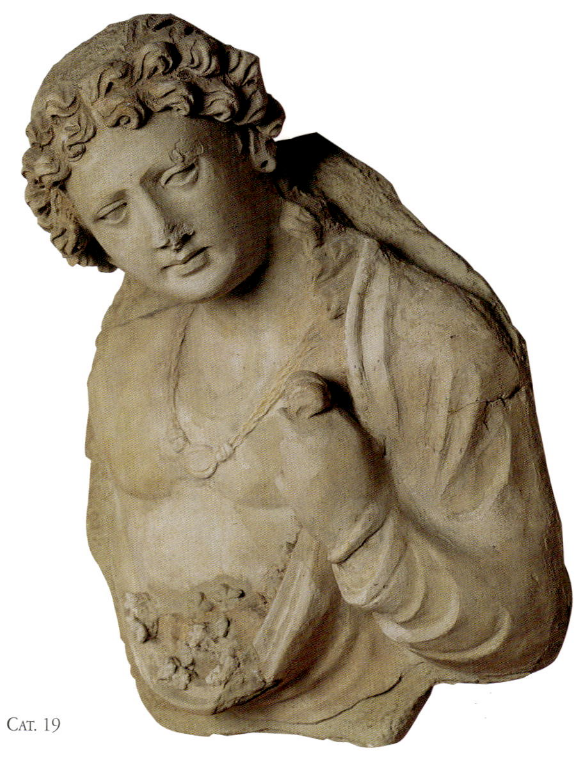

CAT. 19

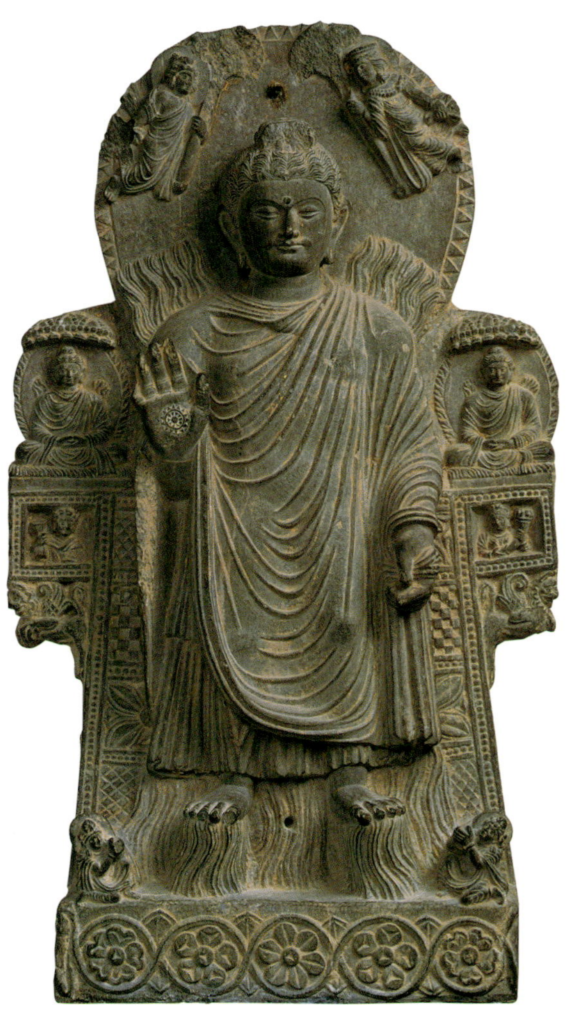

CAT. 18

19

Genie with Flowers

Afghanistan, Hadda, Tapa Kalan monastery
4th–5th century
Stucco; h. 21⅛ in. (55 cm)
Musée Guimet, Paris MG 17190

This figure of a *deva* or genie was found in 1927 in an alcove decorating a courtyard of the Tapa Kalan monastery at the Hadda site in eastern Afghanistan. Through its classical composition, it brings to mind the portraits of Alexander from the Hellenistic period. It represents one of the individuals from Buddhist lore who are frequently found in Buddha's shadow, honoring the master by throwing him flowers, held in one of the folds of the figure's garment, which falls in an elegant curve to the height of his abdomen. The very pure profile, high forehead, and naturally curly hair place this person in northwestern India, not only through the theme and the details of the necklace gracing his chest, but also because of the somewhat limp grace, the full cheeks and rounded oval of the face, and the overly sweet charm; the profile's elegance contrasts with a certain clumsiness in the rendition of the bust or the left hand.

With his slightly bent head and obliquely positioned bust, this princely young man stood out from the wall, the head almost a sculpture in the round, according to an illusionist method inherited from Greece. The *Genie with Flowers* is characteristic of the Afghan school, where stucco progressively replaced schist in the fourth through the fifth century, revealing a juxtaposition of various styles and influences with very strong Greek overtones—stronger than in Gandhara itself. This extremely pronounced Western influence could only have been reinforced, in these regions south of the Hindu Kush, through the ongoing circulation of models or small bronzes of Mediterranean origin, of which traces remain at ancient sites in Afghanistan.

P. C.

ished scene and strike us because of their suppleness and slenderness, the double movement of advance and retreat, and the sweet grace of their charming profiles. They belong to the group of young monks found in Hadda in 1927, from the Afghan school active in the fourth through the fifth century, when stucco replaced schist in surprisingly varied styles. There, the extraordinarily pure Greek influence mixes with distinctly Indian contributions. These little monks, with their fine silhouettes, their well-proportioned waists, and their adolescent, slightly effeminate look, illustrate one of the three gems of Buddhist thought, which places the community of the faithful, most importantly the monastic community, next to the Law and the Buddha himself. Through this grasp of the art of sketching, portraying attitudes that capture life so naturally, the Hadda artists demonstrated a realism that is uniquely theirs.

P. C.

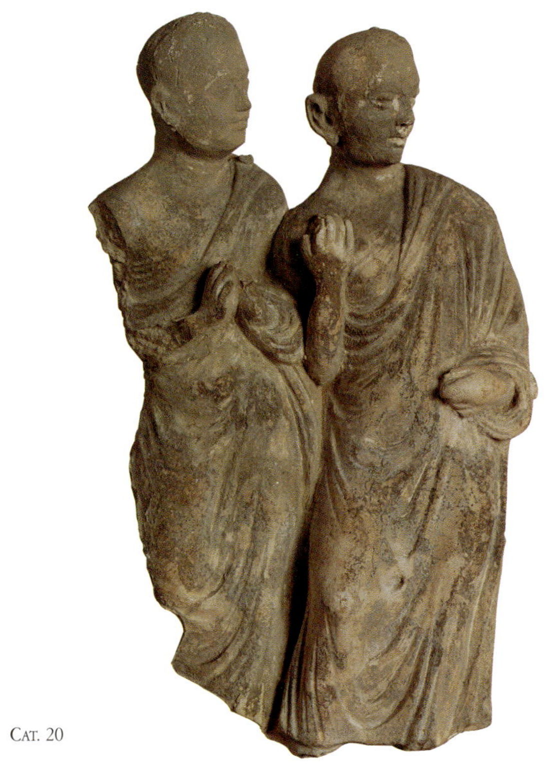

CAT. 20

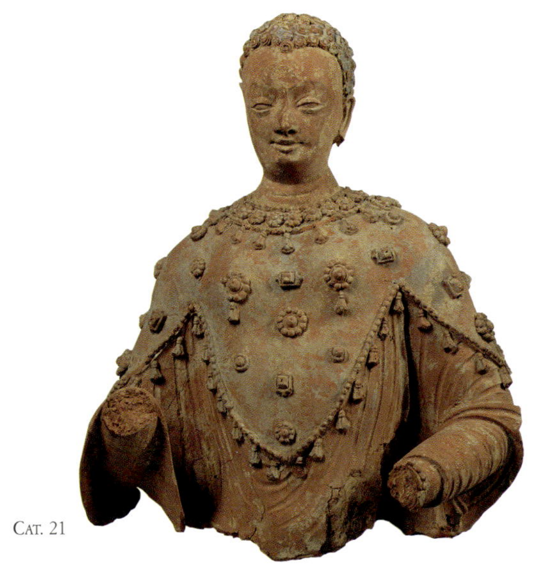

CAT. 21

20

Two Young Monks
Afghanistan, Hadda, Tapa Kalan monastery
4th–5th century
Stucco; h. 9½ in. (24 cm)
Musée Guimet, Paris MG 17233

These two young monks, heads shaven and beardless, come from one of the numerous little votive stupas in the large courtyard of the Tapa Kalan monastery at the Hadda site in eastern Afghanistan. Standing slightly oblique, right shoulders pointing forward, they were part of a now van-

21

Ornamented Buddha
Afghanistan, Ghorband, Fondukistan monastery
7th–8th century
Clay, traces of pigments; h. 20⅛ in. (51 cm)
Musée Guimet, Paris MG 18960

With his childlike face, rounded head and curly hair, delicate posture, and extremely fine facial features, this *Ornamented Buddha* dates back to the end of the Buddhist period in the art of Afghanistan, when a certain mannerism, favoring line, vivid colors, and very soft and often slender forms—a supple and deliberately elongated silhouette—is evident. The Buddha wears a very elaborate three-pointed hood decorated with gems. If the origin of this piece is still uncertain—even though, in the opinion of some scholars, it is inspired by Byzantium—the fact that the Buddha wears this adornment proves that the Buddhist system has now changed, progressively passing from the ideal image of a monk, an ascetic being, to a more worldly, aristocratic atmosphere, with an ornamented Buddha dressed like a prince in the middle of a decor that may symbolize his monarchic, even cosmic powers. Excavated in 1937 from an alcove of the so-called Fondukistan monastery—a Buddhist foundation in the Ghorband valley in the heart of the Hindu Kush—this Buddha sat enthroned on a lotus at the foot of which emerged two small *naga* kings in the middle of a pond [cat. 22]. The figure's hair was painted blue, with the red clay enhanced by touches of paint.

P. C.

22

Two Naga Kings Emerging from a Pool
Afghanistan, Ghorband, Fondukistan monastery
7th–8th century
Clay, traces of pigments; 15¾ x 23⅝ in. (40 x 60 cm)
Musée Guimet, Paris MG 18957

These two *nagarajas* (serpent kings), recognizable by the snakes adorning their hair, emerge from a pool with only their busts visible on either side of a lotus stem, now lost. The group was excavated in 1937 at the Fondukistan monastery, where it decorated one of the side walls of a chapel that was about three feet wide. The *Ornamented Buddha* [cat. 21] sat enthroned on the lotus, wearing a three-pointed hood. The extremely precious Fondukistan style is

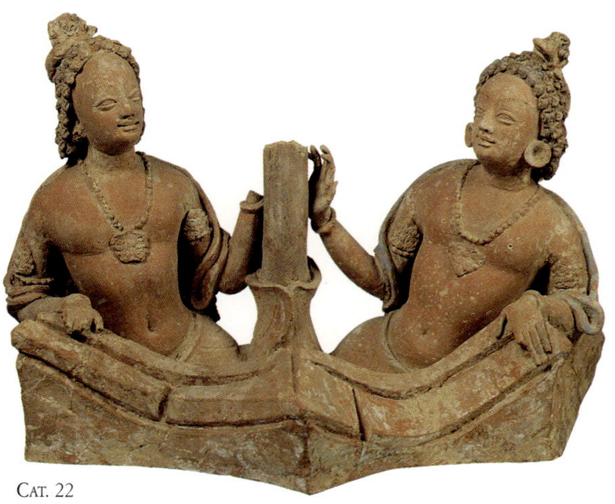

CAT. 22

characteristic of the mannerism prevailing at that time in Afghan territory, when Buddhist art seems to have shown its ultimate splendor, against a background of influences from Central Asia and the vast empire of the western Turks.

These two small *nagas*, with their English-style long curls, their wide-open eyes, surprisingly large earrings, floral-motif pendants, and shoulder bracelets, reflect a quasi-"feminine" aestheticism, essentially playing on the supple forms, soft lines, and fresh colors with very vivid red and blue overtones. The gesture of the hands, with the excessively fine fingers lightly touching the lotus, symbolizes by itself the spirit of a style glorifying refinement and striving for the elegance of a very aristocratic silhouette. The material—unbaked clay modeled over a wooden core—succeeded Gandharan schist and stucco from Hadda, already showing a Central Asian influence as well as a taste for an increasingly "easier" execution.

P. C.

23

Devata Seated at Rest
Afghanistan, Ghorband, Fondukistan monastery
7th–8th century
Clay, traces of pigments; h. 28⅜ in. (72 cm)
Musée Guimet, Paris MG 18959

This *devata* (deity), with his very slight smile and somewhat suave grace, is typical of Afghan art from the seventh century and comes from the Fondukistan monastery. There, in 1937, Jean Carl unearthed a courtyard with a small stupa, surrounded by chapels; each chapel housed a group or a figure, and this *devata*, seated at rest, occupied the same alcove as cats. 21 and 22, to the right of the bodhisattva, the main image. Sitting in an oblique fashion, the *devata* shows his profile and, in an almost limp gesture full of abandon, points with his extraordinarily fine fingers toward the central figure.

The post-Gupta-period mannerism and Indian influence constitute the originality of Fondukistan art, whose main purpose is to please. This *devata* exemplifies a style where the material is now clay and where the artist favors supple movements, a very fluid line, and somewhat limp modeling. The figure has kept its paint, with vivid and extraordinarily fresh colors. Upon excavation, when he first appeared with his extremely white complexion and his eyebrows and pupils emphasized by a black line, he seemed

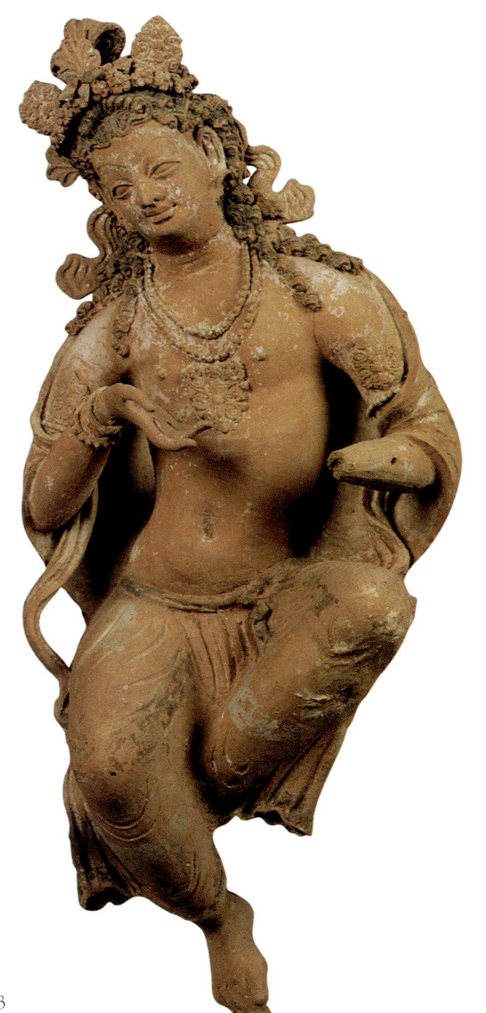

24

Tiara of a Buddhist Officiant
Nepal, 1145 (Nepal Samvat 265)
Inlaid gilded copper; 10 ¾ x 8½ in. (27.2 x 21.5 cm)
Musée Guimet, Paris MA 4929

This tiara is made of embossed pure copper plates. Some have been cut out in fleurons and pierced. The top of the headpiece, ornamented with a half diamond-thunderbolt (*vajra*), has been cast using the lost wax method. Parts of the inlaid semiprecious gems that decorated the work are still visible.

In Nepal, this type of tiara was worn by the tantric masters during ceremonies. Its shape brings to mind the buns worn by some supreme bodhisattvas and the Buddhas with whom the officiants identify. The five main fleurons are decorated with five jinas or "victorious" Buddhas, in perpetual meditation, spread around the headpiece as if on a meditation diagram, or mandala. Each one is associated with an area in space and makes his own characteristic canonic gesture.

An inscription in Sanskrit on the lower band lists a date corresponding to 1145.

N. B.

"surprisingly alive." The figure is wearing a simple *dhoti* in Indian fashion, with traces of blue coloring, and a scarf nonchalantly thrown over his shoulders. Contrasting with this apparent simplicity, the elaborate hairdo and purely decorative jewels show a deliberate mannerism and a refined and precious taste. A wide face with regular features is framed by the hair tuft gathered in a bun (similar to some Gandharan bodhisattvas), a flower garland emphasizing the carefully combed hairdo, English-style curls dropping on the shoulders, and floating ribbons inherited from Iran. The small and slightly mischievous mouth, straight nose, and almond-shaped eyes suggest an ideal beauty with feminine charm.

P. C.

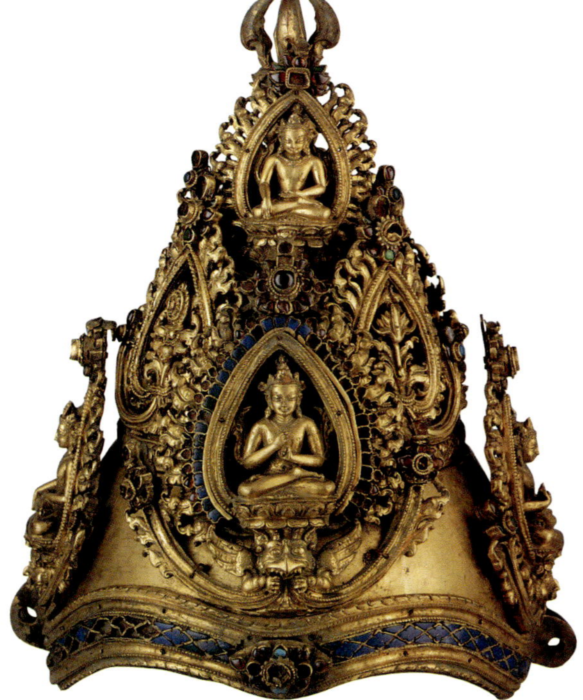

CAT. 24

topped by the Book of Perfect Wisdom and the sword cutting away ignorance. The image could have been part of a triad composed of a Buddha flanked by two assistant bodhisattvas.

The work has been executed in a practically pure copper; the significant amount of gold present in the metal may have been added voluntarily as an offering. The encrustations, some of which have disappeared, consist of glass as well as lapis lazuli and garnets.

N. B.

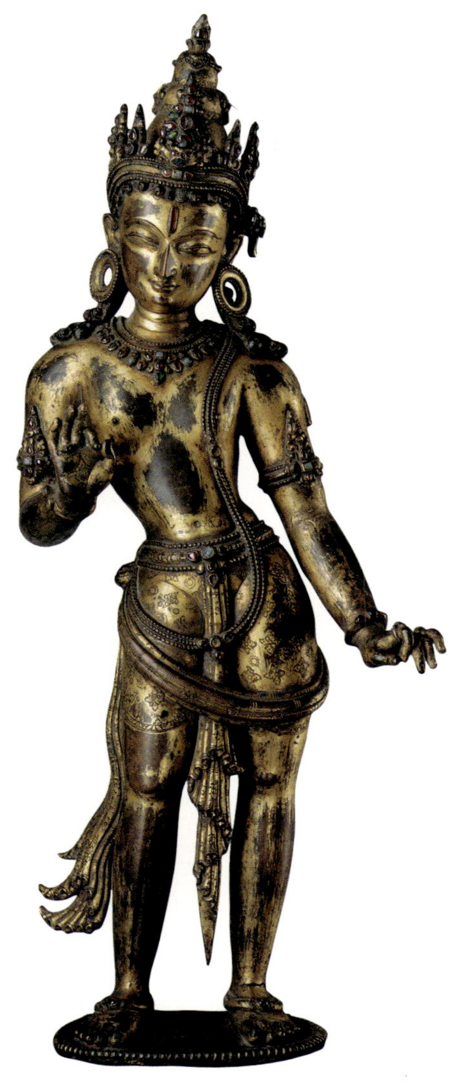

CAT. 25

25

Manjushri?
Nepal, 13th century
Inlaid gilded copper; h. 22 in. (55.9 cm)
Musée Guimet, Paris MA 5031

This large, refined image of a bodhisattva is a remarkable example of Newari metallic statuary at its apogee during the first part of the brilliant reign of the Malla dynasty, between the thirteenth and fifteenth centuries.

The bodhisattva, with gracefully swaying hips and the body in thrice-bent (*tribhanga*) position, makes the gesture of argument (*vitarkamudra*) with his right hand. His left hand held the stem of a lotus, now lost; the arm still shows traces of an anchoring element. The figure could represent the bodhisattva of wisdom, Manjushri, with whom the gesture of argument has been associated. The flower held in the left hand would, in that case, have been a blue lotus, perhaps

26

Queen Maya Devi Giving Birth to Prince Siddhartha
Nepal, early 19th century
Inlaid gilded copper and brass; h. 21½ in. (54.5 cm)
Musée Guimet, Paris MA 1779

Queen Maya, the first spouse of King Suddhodana, ruler of the Shakya confederation, gives birth to Prince Siddhartha, the future Buddha Shakyamuni; she stands in the *tribhanga* position and holds in her raised right hand a

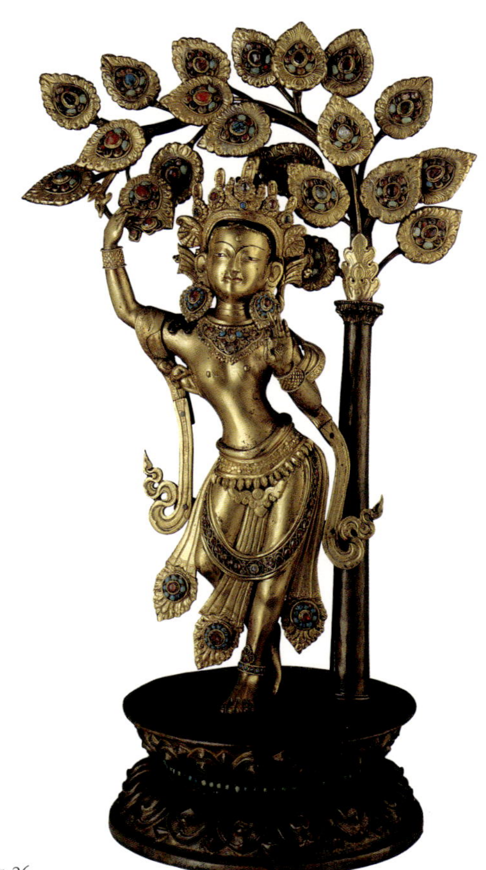

CAT. 26

flowering branch of a sala tree. So as not to be soiled, the child, hands joined in tribute (*anjali*), comes out of his mother's right side "without wounding her." According to tradition, the episode took place in the Lumbini park, in the Nepalese Terai. The work is indicative of the duration of the influence of Indian traditions in Nepal. The Musée Guimet piece stands out as one of the most beautiful representations of this subject during Nepal's late period.

The technical virtuosity of this piece, sumptuously decorated with multiple semiprecious stones, and the sense of movement, are characteristic of the artistic production of the first half of the nineteenth century. During that period, when the Ghurkas reigned, the shops of the bronze workers were still prosperous in spite of the fall of the Malla kingdoms in 1769.

N. B.

27

Avalokiteshvara Appearing as Sugatisamdarshana?
Kashmir, early 11th century
Brass inlaid with silver, traces of pigments;
h. 13⅛ in. (33.4 cm)
Musée Guimet, Paris MA 5943

The production of metallic statuary in Kashmir, the region linking India with Tibet, was particularly important during the medieval era (from the eighth to the thirteenth century).

This six-armed image of Avalokiteshvara evokes the form of Sugatisamdarshana, "observer of the good ways (of reincarnation)." The bodhisattva holds a rosary in a right hand, a ewer and the stem of a fully blooming lotus in two of his left hands, and wears an antelope skin bound around his chest as well as the image of Buddha Amitabha, jina of the West, in one of the points of his tiara, all elements that are usually associated with him. The solid metal statuette has retained several polychrome elements: lapis lazuli covering the hair; vermilion in the right corner of the lips; black pigment lining the contour of the eyes, eyebrows, and pupils; gilding applied on the face and forehead; and silver encrustations decorating the eyes.

The remarkable delicacy of the facial features and naturalistic rendering of the torso belong to the tenth century, whereas the elongated silhouette emphasized by the nimbus

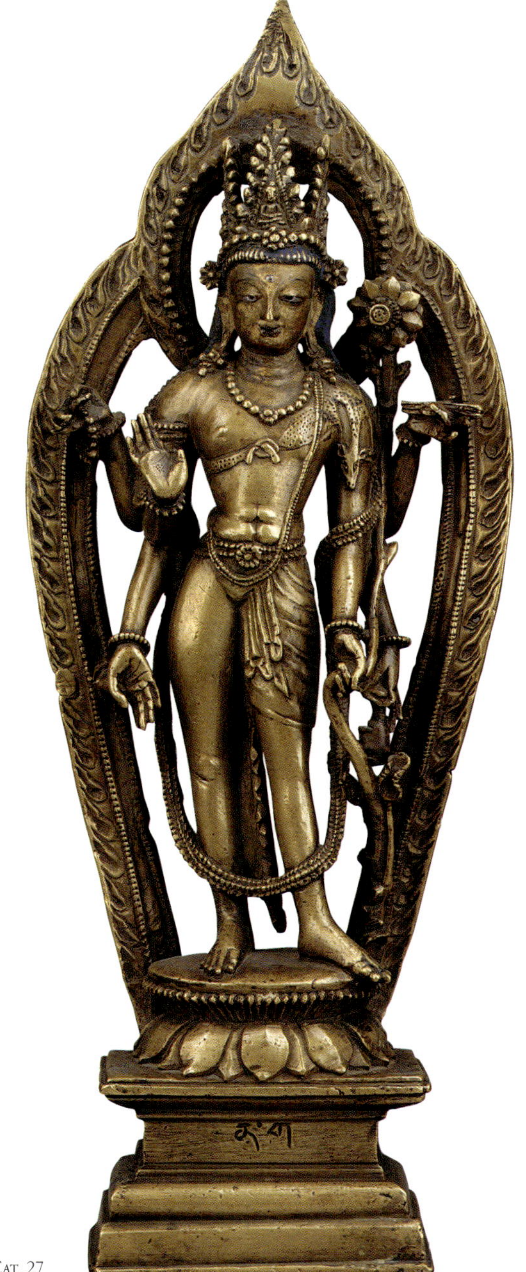

Cat. 27

and flaming halo with the pointed top, as well as the tiara with elongated fleurons, point to the production of the following century.

This work was preserved for a time in western Tibet, close to Kashmir, as attested by the carved name of the donor, one of the sons of the ruler of this region at the time the piece was executed. The statuette is testimony to the importation of Kashmiri pieces to western Tibet during the second propagation of Buddhism and to the role they played in the artistic development of that country.

N. B.

44

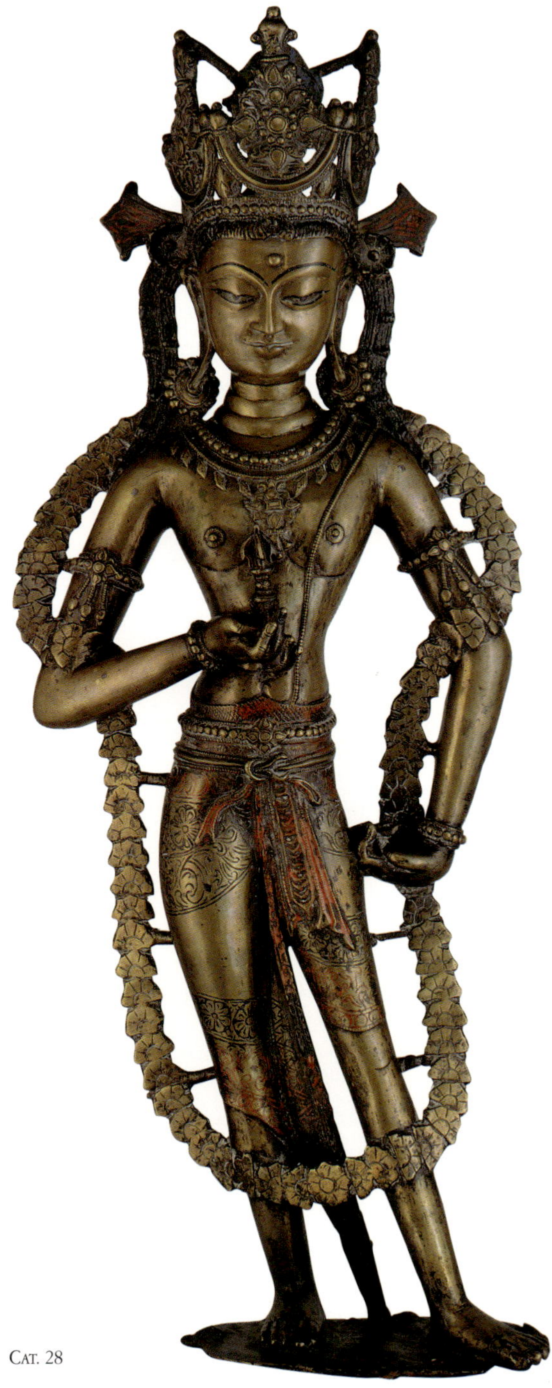

28

Vajrapani

Tibet, 11th–12th century
Inlaid brass with traces of pigments;
h. 27⅜ in. (69.6 cm)
Musée Guimet, Paris MA 3546

The bodhisattva Vajrapani, "bearer of lightning," is very popular in Tantric Buddhism due to his emblem, the diamond thunderbolt (*vajra*), a fundamental principle of this

Buddhist movement, which is present in most rituals. The bodhisattva is standing in a frontal position, his body weight elegantly resting on the right leg. The proportions of the bust and head, more important than those of the legs, were probably meant to correct the effects of perspective, since the piece was, in all probability, perched on a somewhat high altar. The right hand held in front of the torso supports the diamond thunderbolt, and the left hand is braced against the thigh.

The strong influence of Kashmiri art is evident in the tiara points decorated with fleurons, the shape of the jewels, the ribbon tied around the hips, the drapery leaving one knee bare, and the flower garland dropping halfway down the legs and tied to the body with small stems. Even the eyes, painted white, evoke the silver encrustations of Kashmiri images. Other details, however, such as the figure's marked elongation, the gestures, and some of the jewelry motifs, which show great originality, tie this sculpture to the art of western Tibet. It was most likely realized during the eleventh or twelfth century, when this prosperous region, supported by monarchs who had made the protection of Buddhism one of the main thrusts of their policy, had close religious and artistic relationships with nearby Kashmir. Cast using the lost wax method, the statue is made of brass, a material widely used in Tibet.

N. B.

29

Buddha Shakyamuni

Tibet, 15th–16th century?
Copper; h. 11⅛ in. (29.5 cm)
Musée Guimet, Paris MA 3539

In Tantric Buddhism, Shakyamuni holds a preeminent place and remains omnipresent. In Tibetan art, following the Indian iconography, the historical Buddha and the various episodes of his last existence are very widely represented.

Seated in meditation and holding the alms bowl in his left hand, which rests in his lap, the Buddha makes with his right hand the gesture that takes the world as his witness, an allusion to the victorious episode during which he proved his immovable will to preach his teachings to the world, facing the assaults of Mara, the god of Death.

The ascetic's garment worn by Buddha consists of squares of cloth that form a sort of quilt evoking the Magadha rice fields in India; according to tradition, the

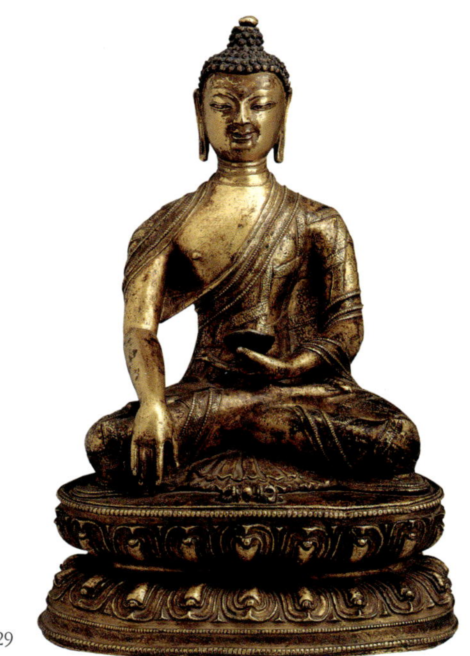

CAT. 29

cloth comes from pieces of shrouds collected at cremation sites or old clothes donated by secular people to the Buddhas and monks. However, these rags are here transposed into a sumptuous garment trimmed with stylized and cutout floral motifs, showing great refinement. The Buddha wears this type of garment in many sculpted and painted representations of the same theme in Tibet, especially in the fifteenth century. A diamond thunderbolt (*vajra*) is lying in front of him and perhaps corresponds to a tantric form of Shakyamuni.

N. B.

arms, and four legs. The divine couple crushes two of the four Mara, Hindu deities; the two others are shown worshipping in the background, while the god's posterior legs are executing dance steps. Nairatmya brandishes a cleaver and a cranial cup, while Hevajra holds sixteen such cups, containing on one side animals, and on the other side seated Hindu deities, their hands joined.

Various elements, such as the elongated proportions, the supple contours, the numerous encrustations, and the jewels, show a marked Nepalese influence; other details, such as the fleurons appearing above the armbands and the garland of human heads, are clearly Tibetan.

N. B.

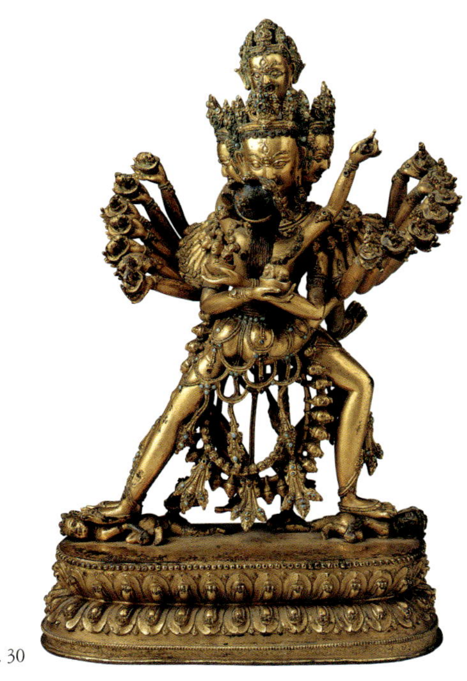

CAT. 30

30

Hevajra and Nairatmya

Tibet, 16th century
Inlaid gilded brass; h. 11¾ in. (29.7 cm)
Musée Guimet, Paris MA 499

Hevajra belongs to the group of guardian deities with an esoteric character who appear in Tantric Buddhism. Personifications of philosophical systems, these deities usually present a fierce appearance. Hevajra, one of the best known and among the most important of this group, has a special place in the pantheon of religious orders.

Embracing his consort, the goddess Nairatmya, Hevajra is depicted in one of his numerous appearances, the widespread Kapaladhara, with eight fierce faces, sixteen

31

Avalokiteshvara Appearing as Ekadasamukha

Tibet, 17th century
Inlaid gilded copper, partly polychromed, h. 9 in. (22.8 cm)
Musée Guimet, Paris MA 1433

Avalokiteshvara, the bodhisattva of compassion, was the object of a very fervent cult in Tibet, of which he is the protector. The Sutra of the Lotus of the Real Law gives him the epithet *samantamukha*, "he who faces everything." This is illustrated by the shape with eleven heads he takes here (Ekadasamukha). Appearing in this manner, he has generally eight or "one thousand" arms, not preserved here, and may be sitting or, more often, standing.

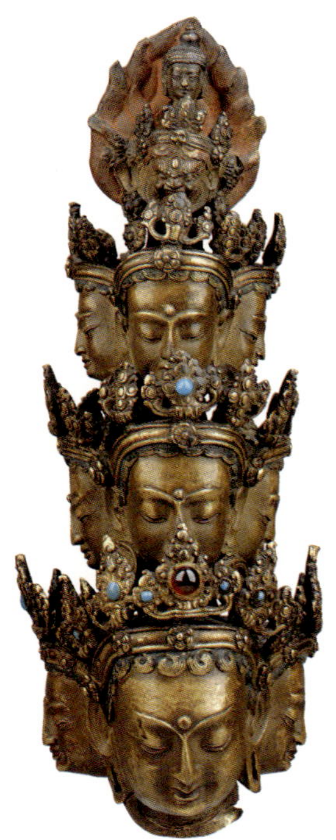

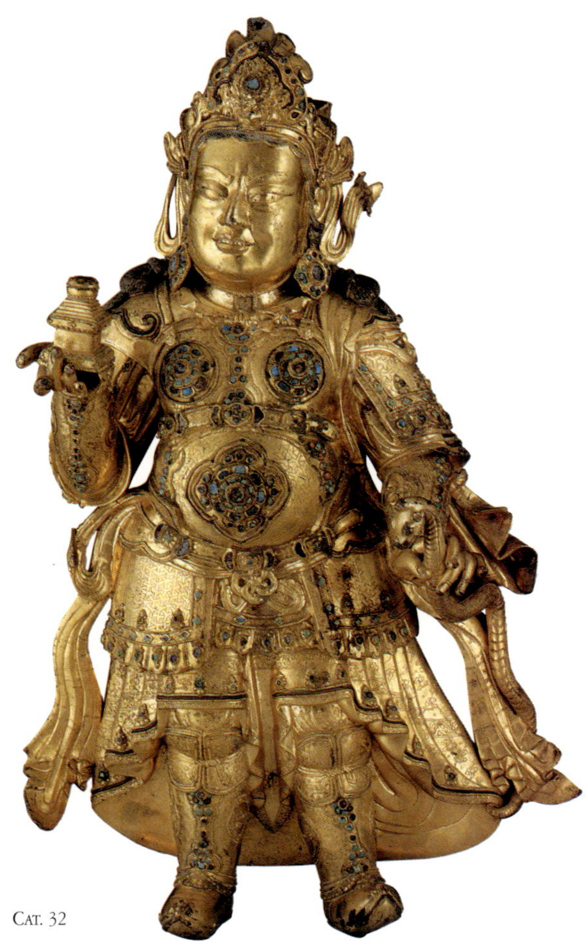

Three tiers decreasing in size, each consisting of three peaceful faces, are superimposed and topped by a fierce-looking head, over which appears the serene face of Buddha Amitabha, "the Infinite Light," of whom Avalokiteshvara is the emanation. These eleven faces correspond to eleven directions (cardinal points, intercardinal points, zenith, nadir, and center); the grimacing face, sometimes considered to be the face of a guardian of the religion (*dharmapala*), is the nadir, and Amitabha's face the zenith. The ten heads, decorated with tiaras with fleurons inlaid with semiprecious gems, represent the ten stages toward enlightenment, here symbolized by Amitabha. These androgynous-looking faces gaze downward, as befits "the Lord who contemplates from above."

N. B.

32

Virupaksa

Tibet, 15th century
Inlaid gilded copper; h. 28 in. (71 cm)
Musée Guimet, Paris MA 4963

Guardian of the West, Virupaksa belongs to a group of four kings who guard the four corners of the world (Lokapala). The first known representations of their cult in historical Tibet can be dated between the end of the eleventh and the fourteenth century.

The representations of Lokapala in Tibet are strongly marked by Chinese influence. They are always in armor, and the Musée Guimet Virupaksa presents variations from the armor of the Tang-period Guardian Kings (618–907), from which it draws its inspiration. The Lokapala iconography evolved over time to become fixed, it seems, during the fifteenth century—the Ming period—in Tibet as well as in China.

Virupaksa's attributes here are a reliquary stupa and a serpent; the former attribute was previously worn by Vaisravana, Guardian of the North. Though possessing fangs, his face is smiling. In spite of his very Chinese appearance, different technical and stylistic elements link this piece to Guardian Kings in southern Tibet, represented on reliquary stupas that were probably built between approximately 1350 and 1550.

The lost wax technique was used to make this pure copper sculpture, mostly hollow with the exception of the scarves, serpent, and hands. Gilded with amalgam, the piece also has encrustations of lapis lazuli, turquoise, pink coral, red and clear glass, and polychrome traces on the lips and hair.

N. B.

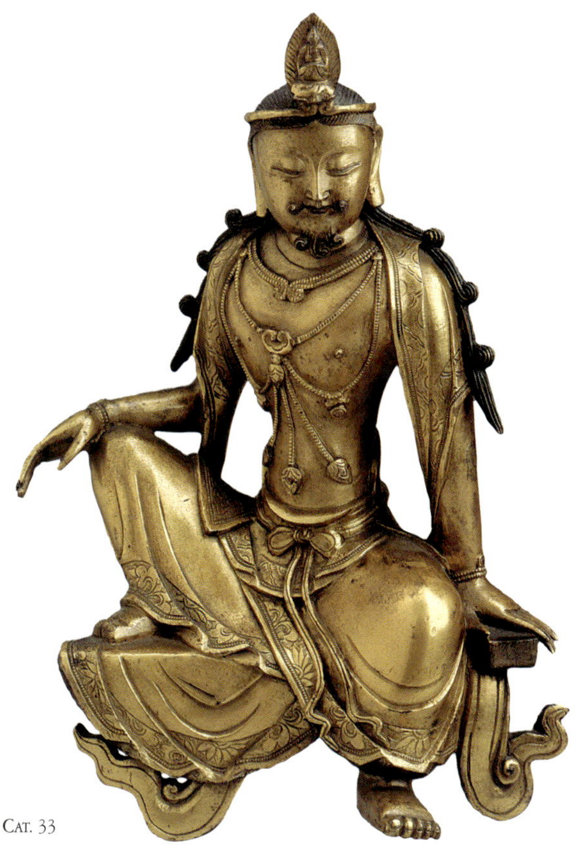

33

Manjushri
China, 18th century
Gilded copper and brass, partly polychromed;
h. 9¼ in. (23.5 cm)
Musée Guimet, Paris MG 10639

From 1260 to 1911, Buddhism was one of the official religions of China. The Qing emperors (1644–1911) encouraged its propagation throughout the empire, with imperial orders being especially numerous under the reign of Qianlong (1736–1795), when Tibetan Buddhism reached its apogee.

Manjushri, the bodhisattva of wisdom, played, in various forms, an important role in Tibet's pantheon. Some of the most preeminent lamas of the country's history were themselves considered to be incarnations of the bodhisattva. Tradition, moreover, states that he resides in northwestern China, on Wutai shan mountain, still today an important place of pilgrimage, which Emperor Kangxi (1662–1722) visited in person several times.

Represented here in the appearance of a young Chinese prince, Manjushri is sitting in a variation of the "royal

relaxation" attitude, his left hand resting on the *Prajnaparamitasutra*, symbol of transcendent wisdom. The jina summarily portrayed at the front of his hairdo has not been identified with any certainty. This iconography, peculiar to Chinese art, represents a close analogy to one of the forms of Avalokiteshvara and was already in fashion between the tenth and the fourteenth century.

N. B.

34

Guardian King (Lokapala)
China, Gansu province, Dunhuang
second half of 8th century
Polychromed wood with traces of gilding
h. 39 in. (99 cm)
Musée Guimet, Paris MG 17761

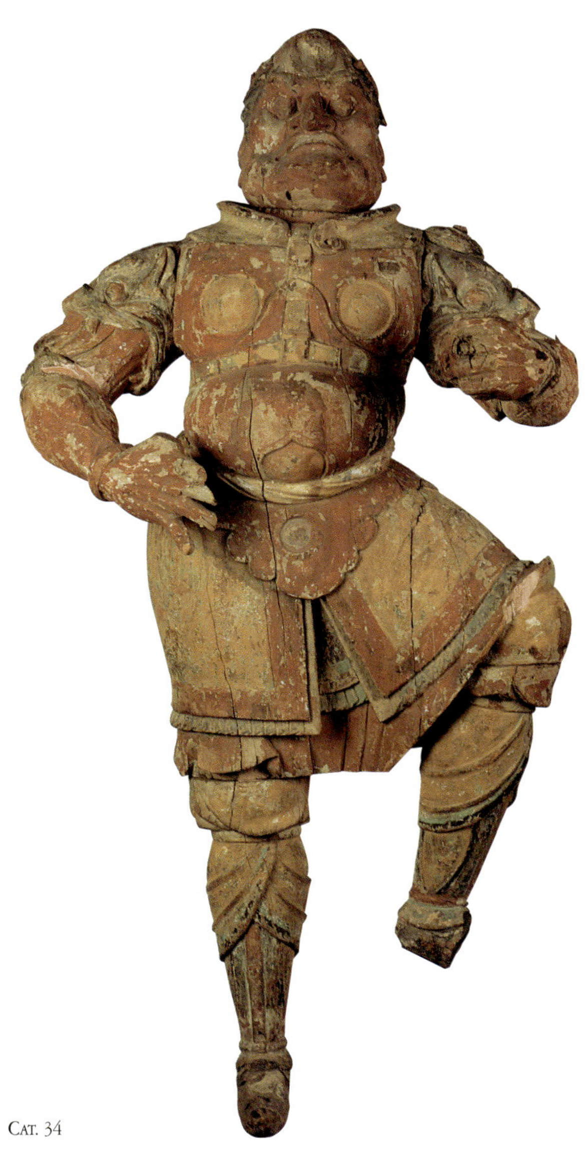

These powerful effigies reflect the Chinese influence that pervaded the sanctuary art of Dunhuang, even in figures that were inherited from the Central Asian world. Such animation, which is expressed by the demonstrative poses and the challenging balance of the statues, by the tension visible in their exaggerated musculature and inflated chests under the armor, and by the caricature of a grimacing face seized by sacred wrath, appears in the statuary and paintings from the high Tang period, extending from 712 to 781. The military garb is a pretext to exhibit a most realistic naturalism, since the depiction of contemporary parade armor is so detailed that it constitutes an exact replica of the pictorial art of that era.

J. G.

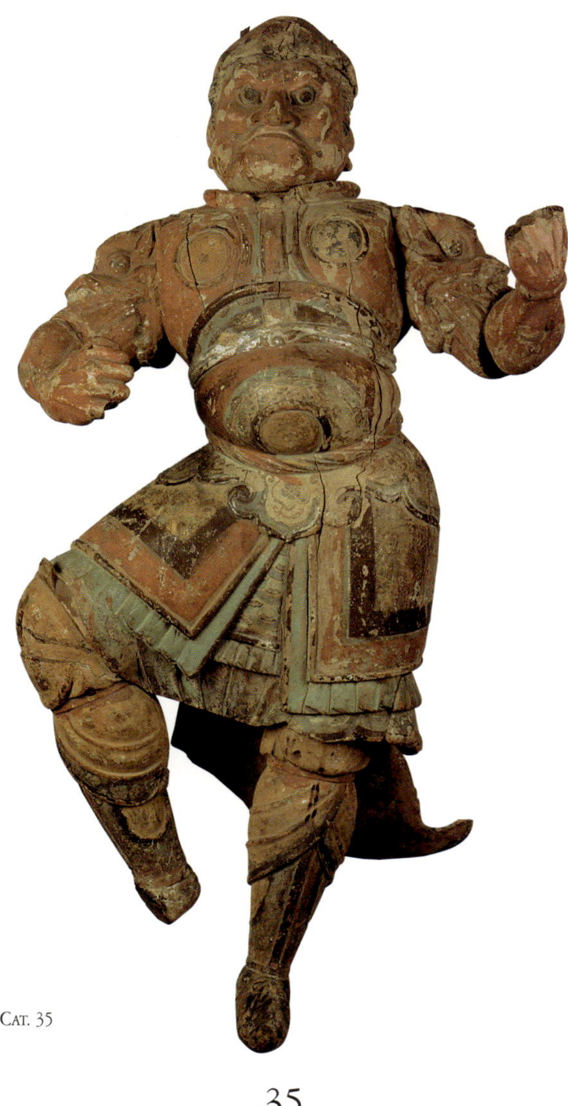

CAT. 35

35

Guardian King (Lokapala)
China, Gansu province, Dunhuang
second half of 8th century
Polychromed wood with traces of gilding
h. 37⅝ in. (95.5 cm)
Musée Guimet, Paris MG 17762

These warrior figures are witnesses of the important religious statuary present in the sanctuary caves of Dunhuang in the Gansu province of northwestern China. Guardian Kings of the Four Directions, their presence in Buddha's entourage is explained by the belief that the doctrine and its preacher must be protected and defended against opposing forces. Consequently, their silhouettes are decidedly warlike, appearing as generals in armor. The role of each one of them is to watch over one of the cardinal points from the celestial height where they reside, on terraces halfway up the cosmic mountain, Mount Sumeru.

36

Head of a Bodhisattva
China, Xinjiang Uighur, Toqquz-Sarai (Tumshuq)
6th–early 7th century
Dried, partly baked clay; h. 11 in. (28 cm)
Musée Guimet, Paris MG 23693

Brought to light by the Paul Pelliot expedition in 1906, the art of the Tumshuq site at Toqquz-Sarai yielded a rich archaeological treasure; in the sixth and early seventh centuries a monastic and cultural center could be found there. This monumental head in dried clay is relatively close to two other very similar heads discovered at the same site, all of which reveal a fundamental trait of the art of the Tumshuq: the extensive use of molds, a clever technique that allowed the reproduction of these faces but remained attentive to variations, such as ornamental details in the hairdo or the important tiara and crown motifs. The modeling of

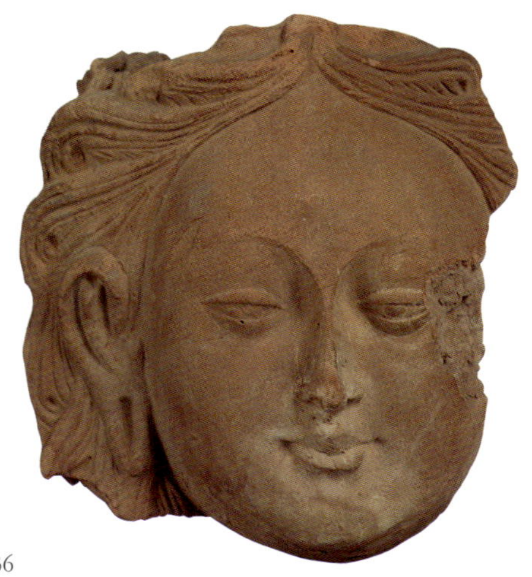

CAT. 36

these heads also explicitly illustrates the later Tumshuq style; formalism emphasizes the oval of the face, whose elaborate features seem to be denser around the bridge of the nose. The eyes are bulging, whereas the arc of the eyebrows is rapidly toned down on the forehead; the mouth has become smaller but retains the half smile characteristic of the ecstasy brought on by the enlightenment.

J. G.

in the middle. The figure is made out of cob and painted in natural colors, rendering a vivid and realistic image of the person.

Next to the figures worshipped in the Buddhist pantheon, such as the bodhisattva and lesser divinities, who were often represented in prayer, a place was set aside for portraits of monks and secular donors. This work points to the art of northern China; stylistically, it brings to mind the works of the Tang dynasty. The Chinese appearance of the figure conforms to the style in Central Asia from the second half of the seventh century and the middle of the eighth century, the final period for the artistic activities of Kumtura.

J. G.

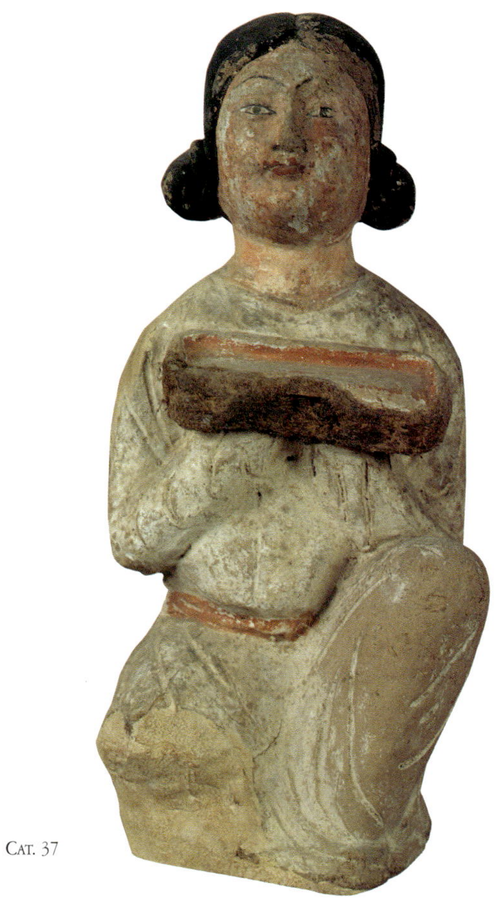

CAT. 37

38

Head of Mahakasyapa
China, Henan province, Longmen
Northern Wei dynasty, early 6th century
Stone; h. 23⅜ in. (59.5 cm)
Musée Guimet, Paris AA 268

This famous head of the great disciple Mahakasyapa comes from the wall of a cave at the Longmen temple complex in Henan province. Dramatically and expressively distorted, the extraordinary composition of this monumental

37

Young Man Kneeling in Prayer
China, Xinjiang Uighur, Kucha, Kumtura
mid-7th–mid-8th century
Polychromed cob; h. 12⅝ in. (32 cm)
Musée Guimet, Paris MG 23759

This little statue found by the Pelliot expedition in the Kumtura caves, in the Kucha complex, manifests the fervor of devotion; the figure presents an offering, of which only the large plate remains between his hands. A representative of the secular world, this portrait of a young boy is recognizable by his hairdo, arranged in two lateral shells with the parting

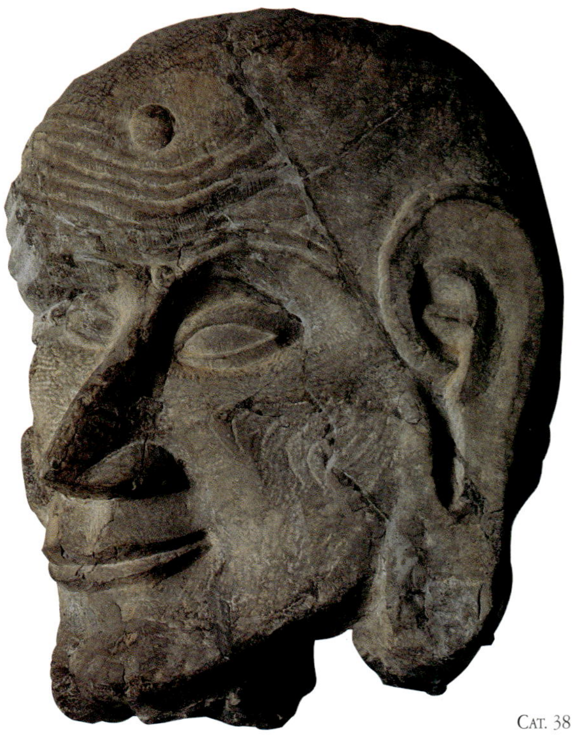

CAT. 38

face of a monk—with its pronounced features stressing maturity, even old age, judging by the wrinkles on the forehead and cheeks—exhibits the characteristics of a low-relief cave painting. Based on the inscriptions, the caves were carved on the order of Emperor Xuanwu of the Northern Wei dynasty, who reigned from 500 to 515.

The work brings to mind other figures of the religious group—of similar dimensions—to which it belonged and, in particular, the main image of the standing Buddha, still visible in the cave and almost treated like a sculpture in the round. The figure of Mahakasyapa is marked by the physical signs of the *arhat* (enlightened being): shaven head and the excessive lengthening of the earlobe, which is part of an ancient Indian formalism distinguishing the exceptional beings of the Buddhist pantheon. The same holds true for the mark on the forehead, a clear analogy with the *urna*, a sign worn by the Buddha. The disciple's body still remains in the cave, entirely draped in a monastic robe and, like the face, depicted in three-quarters profile, turning toward the gigantic Buddha.

J. G.

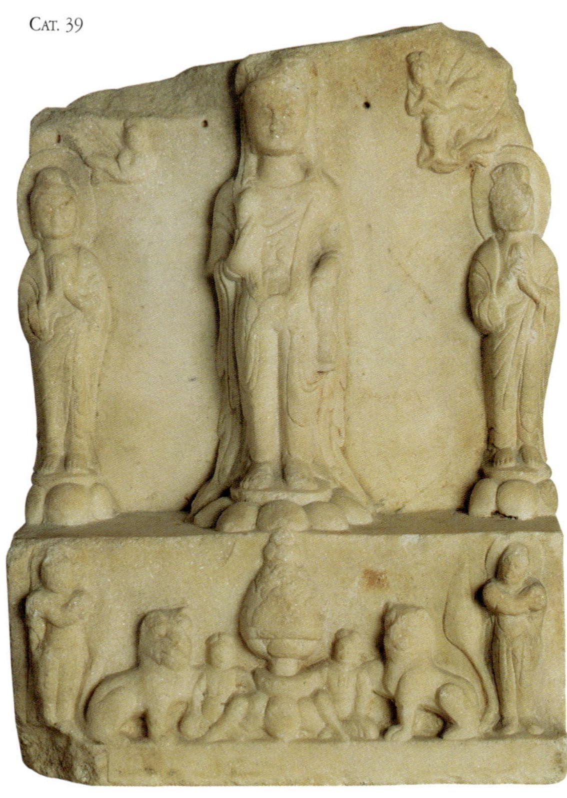

39

Bodhisattva Avalokiteshvara (Guanyin) Triad

China, Northern Qi dynasty, dated 551
White marble; h. 16⅞ in. (43 cm)
Musée Guimet, Paris EO 2765

This rare white marble stele represents a transitional style between the Northern Wei and Tang periods, announcing new religious ideas in a manner that is, in many respects, unique compared to what came before.

Presented as a votive offering, this work depicts a triad of the bodhisattva Avalokiteshvara (Chinese, Guanyin)—recognizable by the attributes of lotus and vase—flanked by two standing figures in prayer, their hands joined in *anjali* tribute and similarly represented on lotus flowers. This work is unique because of the character given to these "attendants" with haloed heads, who are clearly illustrations of Buddhas rather than the usual evocations of lesser-ranked bodhisattvas; they are draped in monastic robes and display the cranial protuberance, the *ushnisha*, which distinguishes enlightened beings. This unusual iconography is purely an invention of the artist.

The accompanying figures, on the other hand, follow faithfully the conventions required for such a group: above the triad are two flying celestial divinities, following the style of Buddhist art of the Northern Wei period. On the pedestal, a relief with the emblematic theme of the adoration and the symbols of the Law appears: in the middle, an incense-burner held by two protective genies in armor, seated directly on the ground (Guardian Kings?); then, following the rules of symmetry, two roaring lions, conventional figures for the preaching of the Law; and, finally, two door guardians complete this composite group on either side.

At the back of the stele appears a dedicatory inscription giving the name of the donors, the purpose of the votive, the temple to which it was given (Baoan), and the date.

J. G.

40

Bodhisattva Avalokiteshvara (Guanyin), Savior from Dangers

China, Sui dynasty, end of 6th–early 7th century
Stone with traces of pigments and gilding;
h. 19⅝ in. (50 cm)
Musée Guimet, Paris EO 2070

Guanyin, one of the most popular bodhisattvas in Chinese Buddhist art, is represented by his own particular

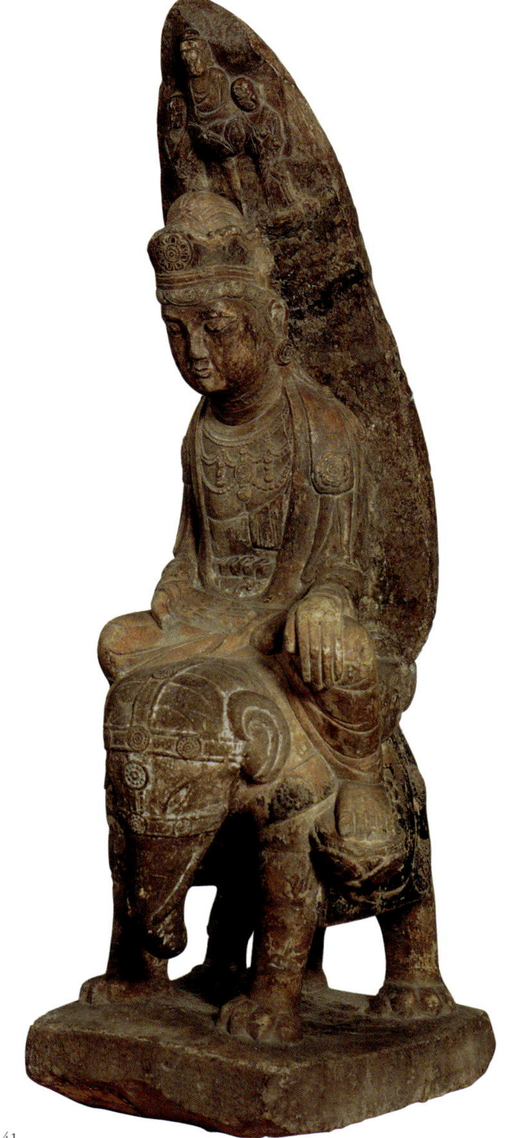

CAT. 40

41

Bodhisattva Samantabhadra (Puxian) Seated on an Elephant

China, Sui dynasty (581–618)
Stone; h. 38¼ in. (97 cm)
Musée Guimet, Paris MG 18624

The bodhisattva Samantabhadra (Chinese, *Puxian*), "universal goodness," is here represented on his mount, an elephant, as described in the Lotus Sutra—one of the first, and maybe even oldest textual evocations describing his powers and how he manifests himself. The text further indicates that the elephant, a royal attribute, is of a fabulous species, white, with six tusks. With the exception of these sparsely provided features, the carved group projects an

attributes. This image—most likely a votive due to the presence of the two donors on the pedestal—clearly illustrates the bodhisattva in his role of "savior from dangers" because of the willow branch that he holds in his right hand together with a lotus stem, another eminent attribute. Based on the famous Sutra of Guanyin, this manner of representing the bodhisattva of compassion, whose powers can prevent and eliminate all dangers, can be found in numerous icons in Dunhuang and other sites in Central Asia.

The figure's physique is a throwback to the "monumental" style of earlier sixth-century art, the Northern Dynasties, and, more precisely, the style of the Sui dynasty. Like other large and small statues with a powerful expression, it retains the aspect of the original stone slab even in the rendering of the long scarf and the massive halo graced with a lotus flower, which is perfectly one with the relief. The figure's rigorous frontality is enlivened by a barely perceptible bending of the left leg. The work exemplifies the masterful art of ornamentation in the draping of the *dhoti* and very detailed, exceedingly realistic jewelry. The face is an ideal mask that fittingly represents the ecstatic expression of the bodhisattva. The presence of two lions on either side of the pedestal symbolizes the preaching of the Buddhist Law.

J. G.

image that conforms to the most popular representation of
the bodhisattva, who has the power to bolster the wishes and
practice of the doctrine through his helpful assistance. This
image is strong and convincing by virtue of its "archaic" fla-
vor. The modeling brings to life an imposing representation
of the bodhisattva, under whom the elephant is depicted
only emblematically, as is the figure holding the animal by
the halter.

Decked out in the rich ornaments of the bodhisattva,
the *dhoti* covering only his legs, and wearing a golden
tiara with the purely ornamental lotus flower motif,
Samantabhadra is seated on his mount in the so-called relaxation pose, the right leg folded, the other hanging down, its
foot resting on a lotus flower. Contrary to most painted
icons, the bodhisattva does not form with his hands the sign
of teaching but keeps his right hand in his lap, the left hand
resting on his knee, gestures that make him appear almost as
if he were meditating. A large, now truncated nimbus above
his head represents a triad of the Buddha treated in high
relief.

J. G.

42

Bodhisattva Avalokiteshvara
(Guanyin)

China, Northern Song dynasty, 11th–12th century
Polychromed wood; h. 79⅞ in. (203 cm)
Musée Guimet, Paris MG 19103

This monumental effigy of Guanyin is one of the most
faithful reflections of the apogee that sculptural expression
reached under the Northern Song dynasty in the tenth
through the twelfth century, the last blazing moments of a
long stylistic and authentically creative process that
stretches back to the great Buddhist style of the eighth and
ninth centuries in the Tang dynasty. Remarkable similarities
can be found between the works of these distinct periods,
whose traits can be recognized throughout the centuries.

The Buddhist art of the Song dynasty, distinct from the
powerful and often superhuman images of the Tang, gives to
this effigy of the bodhisattva of compassion, one of the most
important and powerful figures involved in rituals, a sensitive and human quality resembling humble meditation.
This quality makes the face, with its powerful features,
much like a portrait, and the same can be said of the realistic ornaments decorating his body: the contours and polychrome colors of the drapery of the Indian *dhoti*, which

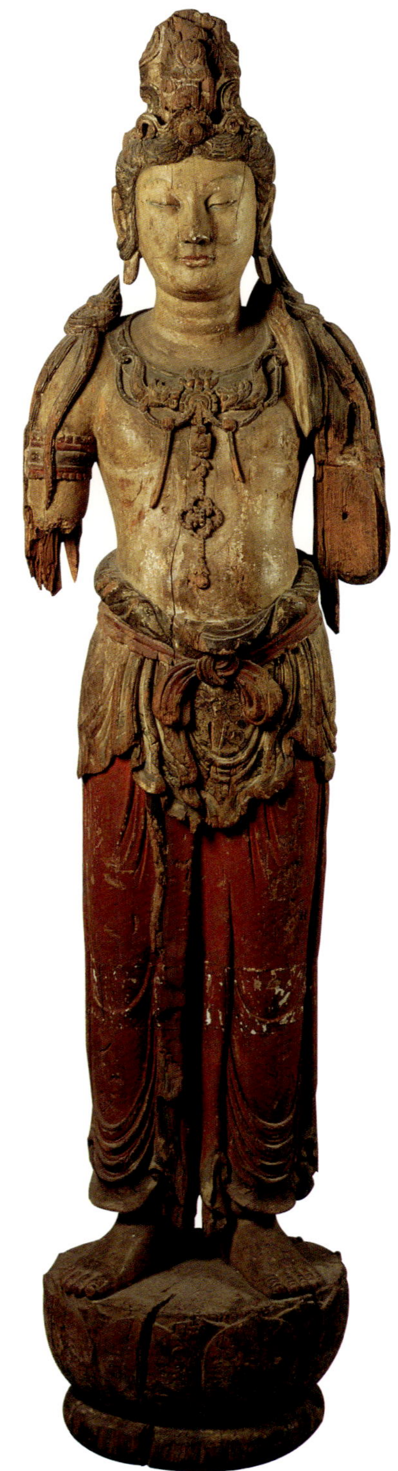

CAT. 42

accentuate the anatomical nudity of the torso, and the
princely finery of both the large golden pectoral and the tiara
placed on the characteristic hairdo, from which escape, in a
clever ornamental design, long locks of hair tumbling on the
shoulders. The motif in the crown seems to be a characteristic attribute marking this great bodhisattva as a Buddha of
Transformation.

J. G.

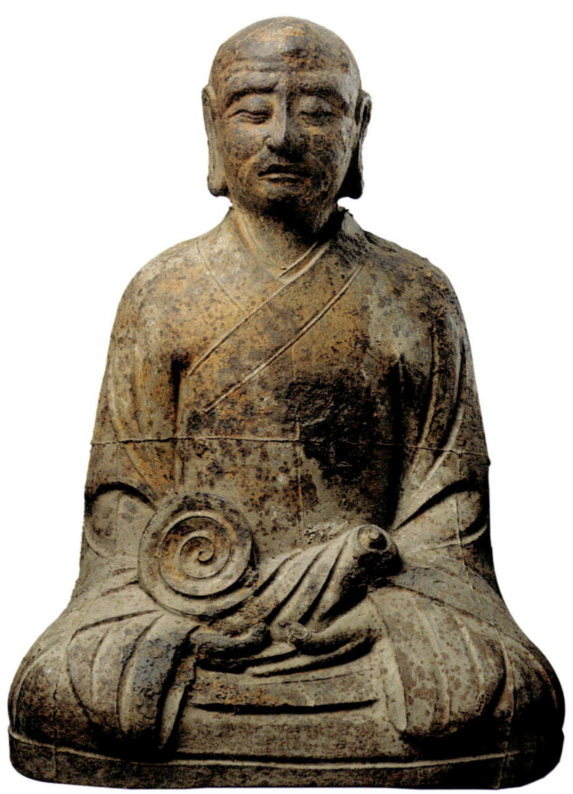

core on the temple altars. The work is living proof that this style continued to be in favor with the Ming.

The raised, partially legible inscription in the cast iron is the dedication from the donors, contemporaries of the Emperor Xianzong (r. 1464–1487) of the Ming dynasty. It mentions an imposing series of *luohan* effigies of comparable style, confirmed by the existence of three other statues dedicated to the same temple. The present statue would have been placed amidst a vast religious group, originally arranged in the temple's main pavilion.

J. G.

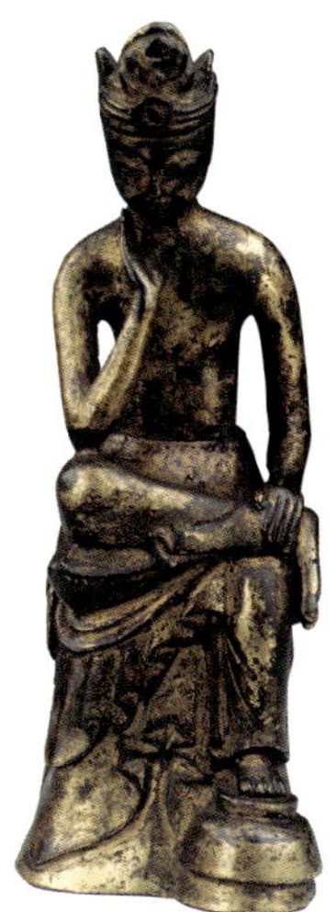

43

Seated Arhat (Luohan)
China, Ming dynasty, dated 1482
Cast iron; h. 31½ in. (80 cm)
Musée Guimet, Paris MA 5949

Saintliness in Buddhism flows from a profound knowledge of the doctrine, which in turn leads to the enlightenment, *bodhi*. Surrounding the Buddha, the pantheon names the deserving beings (*arhat*, or *luohan* in Chinese) who were identified with the great disciples of the first community. Originally there were eighteen *great arhats*, but in certain traditions this list came to include newly worshipped figures in order to reach the symbolic number, considered as countless, of five hundred *arhats*.

This Chinese statue of a seated *luohan*, a sutra scroll opened on his legs, which are crossed in the lotus position, has the peculiarity of being made of cast iron, reflecting the style of the Ming dynasty (1368–1644). The deliberately rough appearance of the raw materials—noticeable by the raised ridges of the cast joints—is typical of a technique dating back to the Northern Song dynasty (960–1127), where pieces were cast in one single stream and erected as a crude

44

The Meditating Bodhisattva
Korea, Three Kingdoms period,
Paekche dynasty, 6th century
Gilded bronze; h. 6⅛ in. (15.5 cm)
Musée Guimet, Paris EO 601

This little gilded bronze recalls the bronze statue at the Seoul Museum, which is unquestionably the greatest masterpiece of Paekche statuary at the time of the Three Kingdoms, when Korea became accessible to influences from China and developed a very personal Buddhist art. This slender-waisted bodhisattva, with his slim extremities, bare chest, and broad shoulders, is depicted in the pensive pose, an attitude whose origin goes back to the Indian art of Gandhara. This pose was transmitted to China under the Six Dynasties and seems to have been especially in favor in ancient Korea; it then passed to Japan during the Asuka period, when the Paekche helped to spread Buddhism within the archipelago.

The poetry and extreme sweetness of the Guimet bodhisattva, with his childlike face and adolescent charm, is characteristic of the southern kingdom that runs alongside the China Sea and which shelters, in a cave in Sosan, a particularly famous triad that includes this same type of meditating bodhisattva, with its pleasing smile and great candor, striking as much for its naturalism as for its kindness and serenity. This bodhisattva, imperceptibly smiling, almost lost in meditation, with his slender silhouette full of elegance, clearly reminds us that Korea at the time of the Three Kingdoms developed an original art and was at the same time an essential stopover on the Silk Road between China and Japan.

P. C.

Charles Varat in 1888, is that of "Avalokiteshvara with one thousand hands and one thousand eyes"—Chonsu Kwanum Posal. This image derives directly from the esoteric Buddhism of the Tang dynasty, which was strongly influenced by Indian iconography. It is the only three-dimensional example of this type of iconography known from such an early date on Korean soil.

The bodhisattva wears a garland of lilies; seated in the *vajraparyanka* position, he bows at the feet of Amitabha, whose figure—held above his head by two of his upper hands—is being presented to the faithful. Avalokiteshvara is the delegate bodhisattva of the "Buddha of Light," the "Buddha with the Endless Life," in whose Western Paradise each creature hopes to be reborn. With his forty-three hands, Kwanum Posal intercedes with this Buddha, whose popularity increased during the Koryo period, which was very troubled by the Mongolian menace. Here he is represented in an omniscient form and truly opens up like the petals of a flower, each hand carrying a different attribute.

P. C.

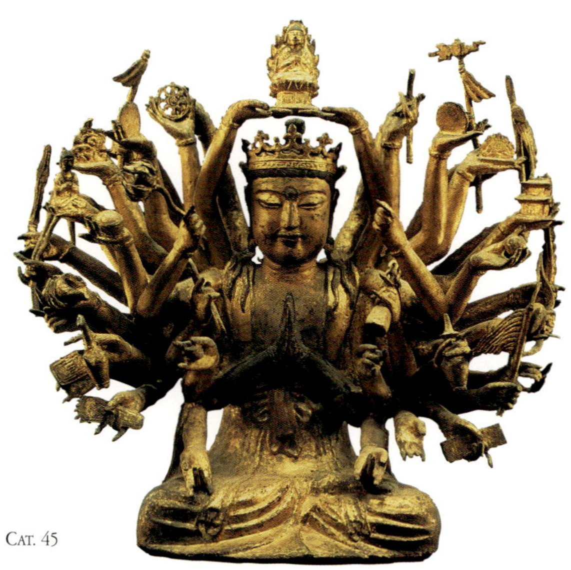

CAT. 45

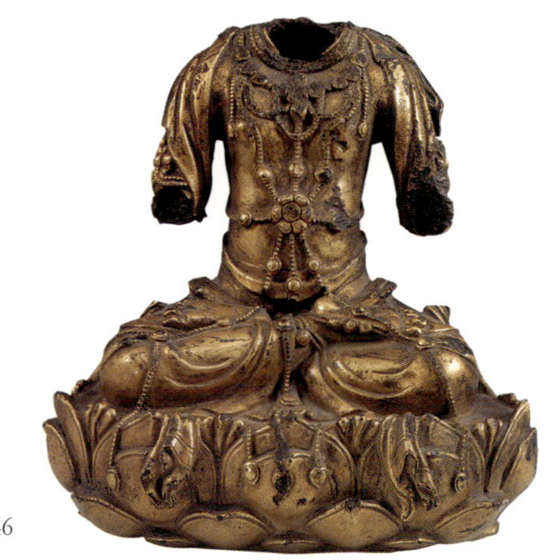

CAT. 46

45

Thousand-Armed Avalokiteshvara (Chonsu Kwanum Posal)

Korea, Koryo period, 10th–11th century
Gilded cast iron; 22⅞ x 24¾ in. (58 x 63 cm)
Musée Guimet, Paris MG 15369

46

Bodhisattva Seated on a Lotus

Korea, Koryo period, 13th–14th century
Gilded bronze; h. 5 in. (12.8 cm)
Musée Guimet, Paris MG 15258

According to the inscription on the base, this spectacular statue comes from Tongbangsa, a temple located in southeastern South Korea. Founded at the time of the Unified Silla Kingdom (668–935) and particularly active during the Koryo period (936–1392), it was destroyed during the Japanese invasion under Hideyoshi, in 1592. Today, only a seven-story stone pagoda remains. The image illustrated by the piece, which was brought back from Korea by

Brought back by Varat in 1888 from the first European expedition in Korea to complete the route by land from Seoul to Pusan, this bodhisattva is one of the most beautiful pieces in the considerable collection acquired at that time. The gilding on this small bronze is perfectly intact.

Headless and with broken arms, the figure is seated in meditation on a lotus with three tiers of majestically opening petals whose origin can be traced directly to the Tang dynasty. Its supple, extremely lively contours are suggested with a great deal of realism. The nude bust is richly adorned, with a great number of jewels and numerous pendants covering the chest and crossing on the abdomen, falling on the legs in natural, simply elegant curves, without giving the impression of overload or overabundance. The fluidity of the overall image is emphasized by the set of scarves covering the shoulders and falling to the pedestal.

This decoration clearly stresses the influence of China on the Korean peninsula during the Koryo period, when Korea, following the Mongolian invasions, had been forced to pledge allegiance to the imperial court of Peking.

P. C.

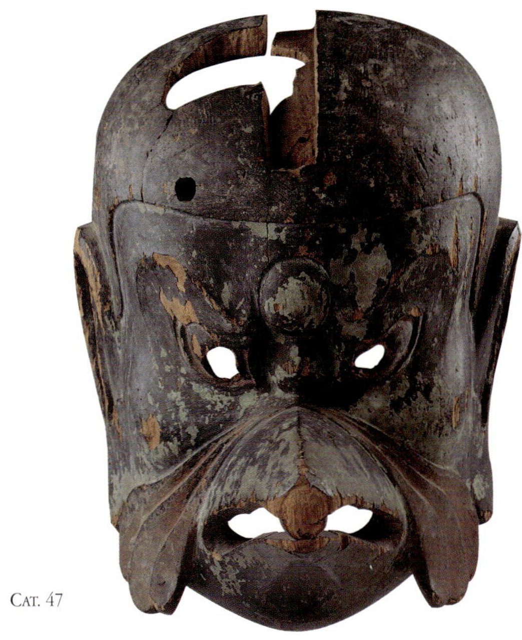

47

Gigaku Mask: Karura

Japan, Late Nara period (710–794)
Lacquered and painted paulownia wood;
h. 11¾ in. (30 cm)
Musée Guimet, Paris EO 643

Gigaku masks are today the only tangible proofs of a dramatic art form that reached its apogee in eighth-century Japan. The Gigaku performances, mixing mime, masked dancers, and music, remained closely linked to the ritual of the great Buddhist temples, in spite of the highly profane character of the drama. Such is the case of this mask, which was worn during the consecration ceremonies of the Great

Buddha of Todaiji in 752. It is carved in soft and light paulownia wood and big enough to cover the face and the upper part of the actor's head; the mask's outer surface is covered with black lacquer applied over a fine layer of gesso. The remaining traces of red and green pigments indicate that it was originally painted in vivid colors, emphasizing its fantastic aspect.

The mask represents Karura, a divine bird from Indian mythology that was accepted into the Japanese Buddhist pantheon as one of the Eight Divinities protecting Buddhism. The fierce nature of this bird of prey is emphasized by a long, crooked beak holding a pearl and framed by red feathers; its bulging eyes are separated by two bumps and hooked eyebrows. The bird's crest has disappeared.

Gigaku masks, through their iconographic and stylistic elements, show not only the influence of China but also of Central Asia, India, or even Greece in establishing this art form.

H. B.

48

Gyodo Mask: Shishiko or Haeharai

Japan, Late Heian-early Kamakura period,
end of 12th century
Lacquered wood; h. 10¾ in. (27.2 cm)
Musée Guimet, Paris EO 519

Though Gigaku representations became rare in the Heian period, certain characteristics of the art form were

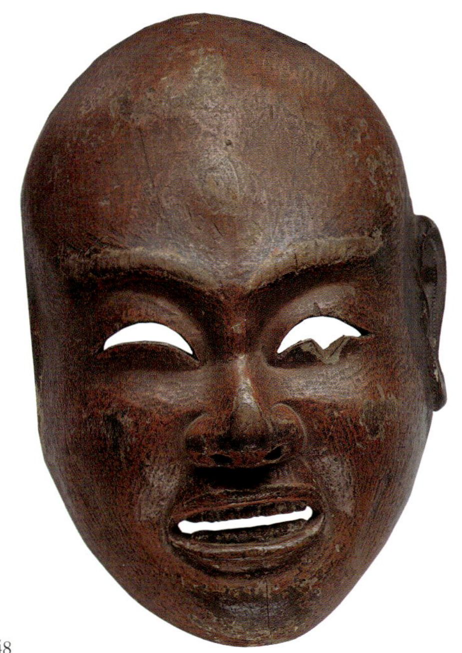

56

kept alive through other forms of masked theater in Japan. The classical "Lion's Dance" opened the Gigaku procession and was also featured in the Gyodo ceremonial processions, with the purpose of warding off evil spirits. A man wearing a lion's head would be flanked by two children (*shishiko*) and escorted by two masked extras (*haeharai*). The physiognomy of this mask is related to similar masks preserved in Japan.

Carved in the dense, textured wood of a camphor tree, the mask is coated with a layer of black lacquer on a fine white gesso layer and finished with a coat of reddish brown lacquer. The eyebrows have been redrawn in Indian ink. The smiling expression of the face, resulting from the stylized line of the very slanted eyes, wrinkles lining both sides of the nose, and the mouth slightly opened on two rows of even teeth, is softened by supple contours. The general impression imparted is that of a youthful and joyous grace, fitting the part especially well. The smaller dimensions of this type of mask are justified by the fact that the part was, in general, played by children, at least in the Gigaku theater.

H. B.

49

Standing Bodhisattva

Japan, Late Heian period, end of 10th century
Cypress wood; h. 65¼ in. (165.8 cm)
Musée Guimet, Paris EO 505

One of the esoteric forms of the bodhisattva Avalokiteshvara that was especially popular during the ninth and tenth centuries, this *Standing Bodhisattva* may represent a Juichimen Kannon (two-headed Kannon); the two smaller heads in the topknot and the metallic crown are now lost. The technique and stylistic traits of this sculpture are typical of a transitional period between the archaism of Early Heian (Jogan) statuary (794–897) and the rise of the Late Heian (Fujiwara) style (897–1185). The so-called split-and-join technique used here is a technical advancement over the mono-block sculpture of the Jogan period; the figure, carved in one single block, has been split vertically in order to hollow out both halves, which are then reassembled.

The work's monolithic aspect and relative bulk make it an extension of Jogan sculpture. The treatment of the details, however, marks the beginning of a more refined style: the garment's drapery, sporadically showing the "undulating wave" lines of the ninth century, hugs the body more closely and brings out less strongly emphasized contours.

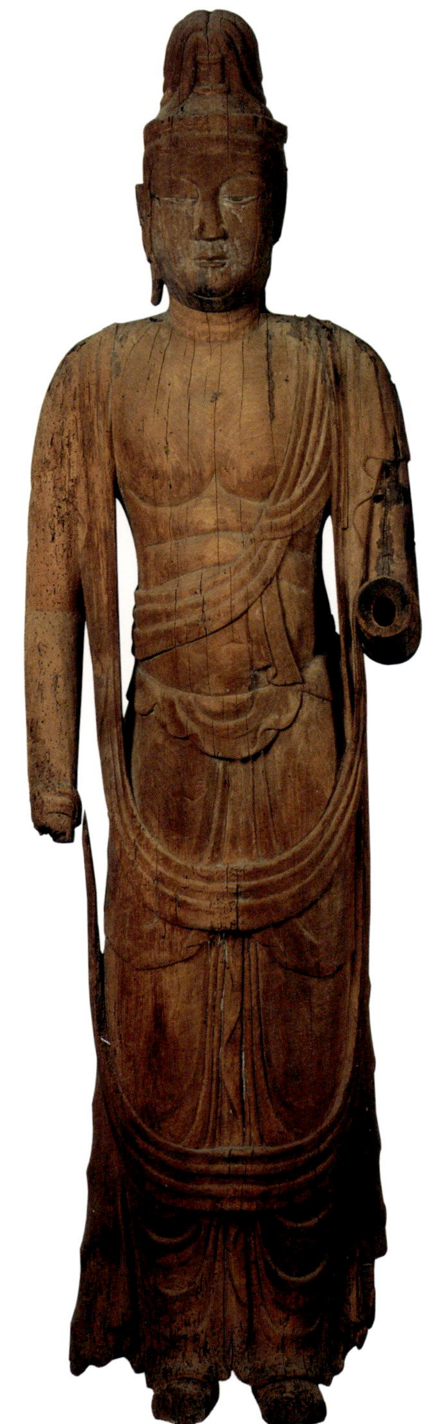

Cat. 49

The contours of the torso and thighs have become softer, and proportions have begun to lengthen. Underneath the stylized seriousness of the face lies a more serene expression, and the transitions between each plane occur in a softer manner. The wood appears in its natural state, except for some traces of white coating, visible in the sunken parts. Originally, it probably would have been covered by a coat of lacquer and gold leaf.

H. B.

57

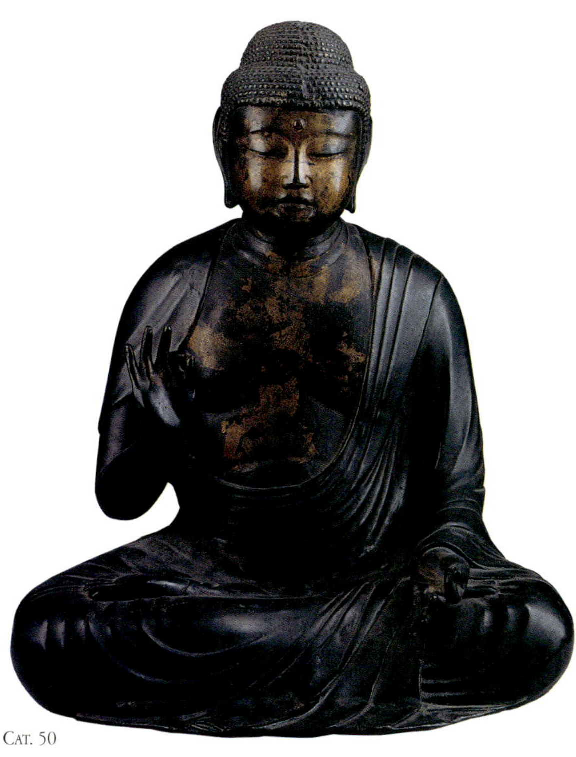

50

Seated Buddha Amida

Japan, Late Heian period, first half of 12th century
Bronze; h. 20⅛ in. (51 cm)
Musée Guimet, Paris EO 1517

This bronze sculpture of Buddha Amida (Sanskrit, Amitabha) is typical of the numerous effigies executed in the eleventh and twelfth centuries, during the Late Heian period (897–1185), when the craze touched off by Amidism and practices such as the "nembutsu"—where the faithful, by endlessly and sincerely invoking the name of Amida were assured rebirth in his Pure Land of the West—produced a wealth of carved and painted images of this great, merciful Buddha. Amidism and the three great Indian sutras that described the Western Paradise ruled by Amida opened up new horizons to the artists of that period in Japan. Amida and his retinue of twenty-five bodhisattvas arriving to welcome the souls of the faithful were endlessly depicted. Here, Buddha Amida makes the so-called gesture of welcome, reserved for the highest class of faithful. Amida is sitting cross-legged, the right leg on top of the left, the right foot resting on the left thigh, in a position used by esoteric sects.

Stylistically, the changes shown in Buddhist sculpture of the eleventh century reflect doctrinal developments and are an expression of new religious ideals. The power and

strictness of the Early Heian style (794–897) gives way, in such images, to a feeling of benevolence and mercy, here expressed in all its purity. This image of Amida, cast using the lost wax method, reaches a balance and an expressive power rarely seen in statues of this size, above all in the features of the meditative face. This face has a dreamy and ethereal expression, soft and compassionate, in conformity with the aestheticism and spiritual expectations of that period.

H. B.

51

Seated Buddha Amida

Japan, Late Heian period, 12th century
Lacquered and gilded wood; h. 32¼ in. (82 cm)
Musée Guimet, Paris

This effigy of Buddha Amida Nyorai (Sanskrit, Amitabha)—whose favorite world is the Pure Land of the West—is especially representative of the new orientation taken by Japanese Buddhist sculpture during the Late Heian (Fujiwara) period (897–1185). The Buddha of Compassion who welcomes the beings to his Western Paradise, Amida is supposed to be the personification of one of the episodes of the historical life of Buddha, when he pronounced his forty-eight-point great vow and promised to save all beings, whoever they may be.

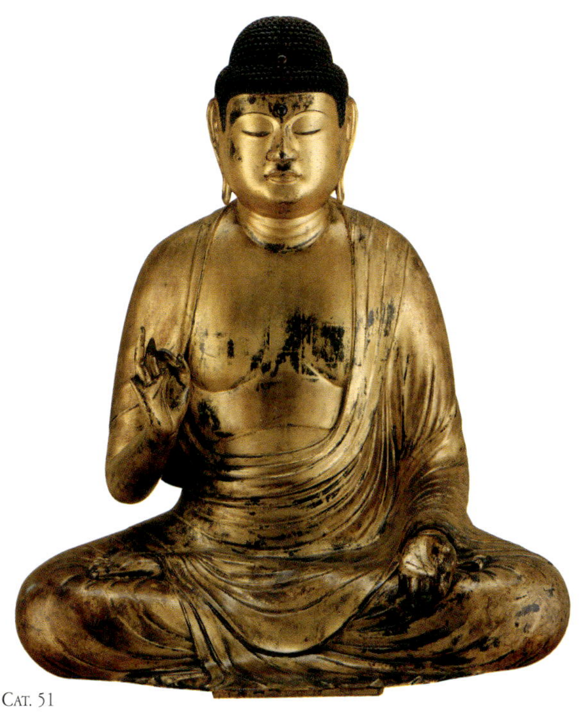

Amida Nyorai is pictured seated, the left leg resting on the right, the hands making the gesture for argumentation. This position, with the thumbs touching the end of the index fingers and forming a circle, corresponds to one of the postures Amida takes when welcoming the faithful to his Pure Land of the West. The *mudra* represented here corresponds to the highest level of welcome, contemplation of the bodhisattva, which is reserved to the faithful who have reached an elevated phase of spiritual perfection. This iconography indicates how much the Pure Land Buddhism was in favor at the Heian court during the eleventh and twelfth centuries.

This sculpture of Amida shows stylistic characteristics developed around the capital during the twelfth century. The controlled technique, combined with a tendency to idealize the forms, produced such images with harmonious proportions and classical balance. The even pleats, sensitive modeling of the bust and arms, and expression of the face— which is at the same time meditative and benevolent—lend a serene beauty to this image, expressed beyond the realm of realism. In the search for elegant forms and softness of expression, which is the trademark of this style in sculpture, the will is also there to represent in a tangible manner Buddha Amida's infinite capacity to show compassion.

H. B.

Cat. 52

right arm hangs straight alongside the body, the right hand resting at the front of the right knee, palm upward in the gesture of giving. This *mudra* of the fulfillment of the wish to devote oneself to the salvation of human beings is, however, more customarily executed with the left hand. Here, the left arm is bent, the three last fingers firmly folded, the thumb covering the index. We may assume that the left hand held a now vanished attribute (lotus flower or lotus vase?), making this a rare form of representation of the bodhisattva Kannon.

H. B.

52

Seated Bosatsu

Japan, early Kamakura period, end of 12th–13th century
Gilded bronze; h. 7⅝ in. (19.5 cm)
Musée Guimet, Paris EO 1494

This bronze figure of a bodhisattva (Japanese, bosatsu) occupies a special place in the history of Japanese Buddhist sculpture: the hollow sculpture has been cast using the lost wax method and can be classified somewhere between a real sculpture in the round and a high relief. Originally this bodhisattva was affixed to the middle of a circular bronze plaque. This quasi three-dimensional representation is characteristic of the Kamakura period. The elongated silhouette, slimness of the torso and arms, and the classicism of the face, with its rather stylized features, suggest a date around the beginning of the Kamakura period (the end of the twelfth to the early thirteenth century).

The rather unorthodox iconography of this bodhisattva makes precise identification difficult. He is sitting in the lotus position, the right foot resting on the left thigh. The

53

Bishamonten

Japan, Kamakura period, end of 13th century
Cypress wood, polychromed and gilded
h. 28⅜ in. (72.2 cm)
Musée Guimet, Paris EO 3100

Among the Four Guardian Kings who protect the four corners of the world and are considered the protectors of the earth and of Buddhist Law, Bishamonten is the Guardian of the North. His attributes are the stupa and the lance.

To stress this entity's ferocious character, he is usually represented as a warrior in armor assuming a fierce pose and trampling a demon. Though this sculpture is small, it perfectly renders Bishamonten's warlike traits: the intense expression of the face is individualized like a portrait; the contracted jaws, firmly closed mouth, knitted brows, and staring gaze communicate a barely contained wrath and ardor. The technically advanced assembly of the piece from multiple, individually worked wooden blocks enhances the expression of movement and body contortions, achieving the

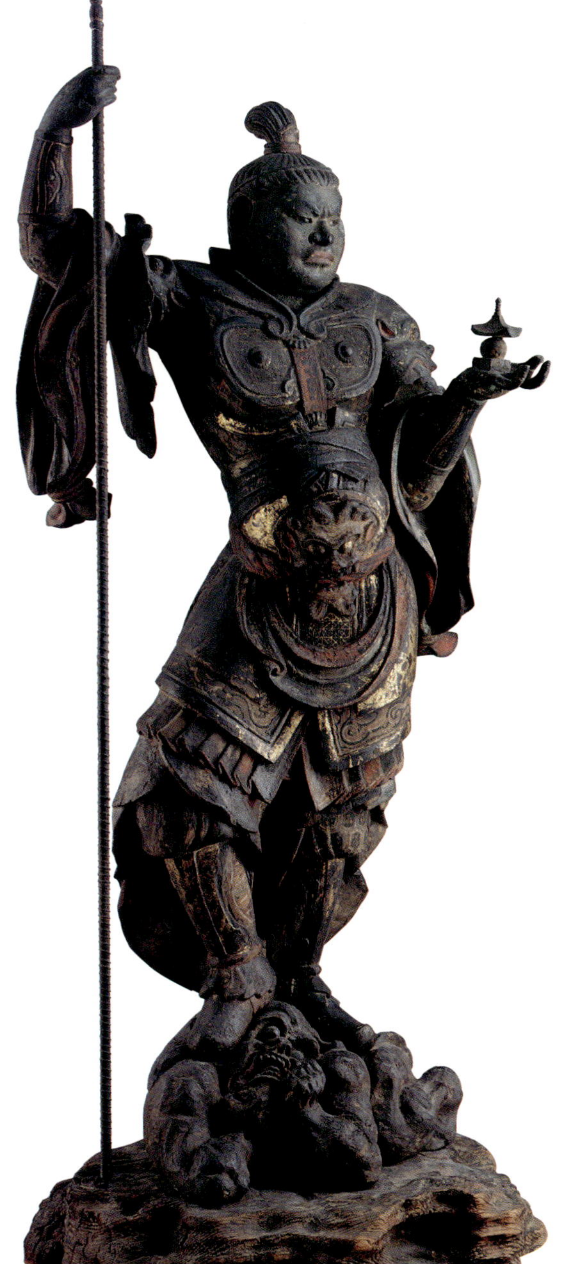

54

Bodhisattva Avalokiteshvara

Vietnam, Trans-Bassac, Tan-Long
Related to Phnom Da style, 7th century
Gray sandstone; h. 65 in. (165 cm)
Musée Guimet, Paris MA 5063

This famous piece, known since 1919, was discovered at Tan-Long, the eastern limit (in its ancient outline) of the vast province of Trans-Bassac, in southern Vietnam, where the Bassac flows into the China Sea. This region of the Mekong delta was Khmer during the pre-Angkor period

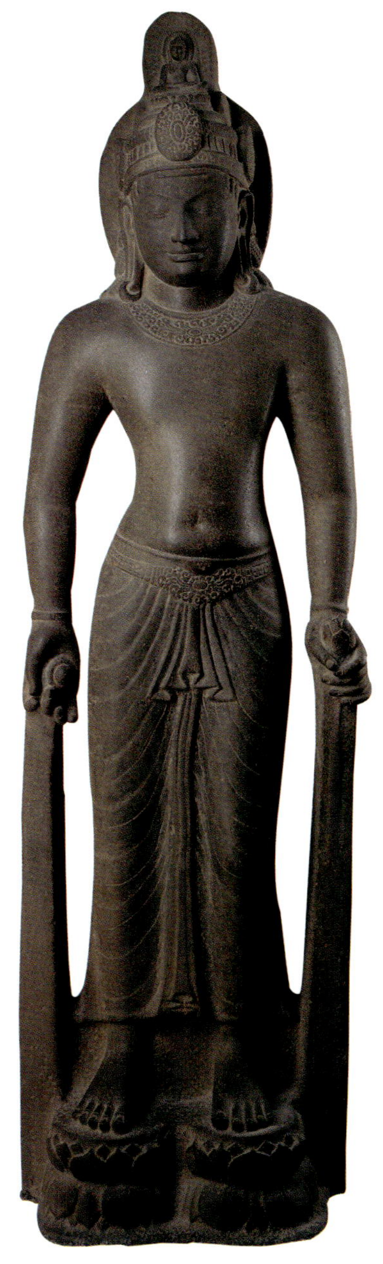

realism that is the trademark of Kamakura sculpture. The figure's dynamic pose—hips swaying, bent right leg pressing down on the demon, raised right arm solidly grasping a lance—is further amplified by the almost baroque treatment of the garment: the sleeves and lower part of the gown seem to flutter in the wind, while the powerful musculature of the torso and shoulders is further emphasized by the breastplate's decorative motifs, in particular three masks of monsters with their mouths wide open. The meticulous application of lively colors and gilded decorations in floral or geometric patterns adds to the sumptuous dimension of this piece.

H. B.

and began to be occupied by Vietnam only in the seventeenth century.

Discovered at a depth of five feet, this very high relief standing against a perforated stele is so well preserved that it is obvious the site had never been reoccupied. The large dimensions are rather exceptional and suggest that the stone was brought from quite a distance. It is possible this Avalokiteshvara formed part of a triad (a Buddha, sitting or standing between two bodhisattvas), but this unusual piece, clad in princely attire, was more likely displayed by itself in its sanctuary.

Discovered in this far southeast region of the ancient Khmer country, about which little is known, this piece appears to have affinities with Indonesian art and even nearby Cham art. The right hand, lowered in a gesture of giving, presents an unusual object that might be a gem, a rare but still possible attribute of Avalokiteshvara, while the left hand holds the predictable lotus. The quality and beauty of the carving, which succeeds in bringing the flesh to life and giving movement to the figure, as well as the sublime expression of spirituality, suggest the sculpture was made under royal patronage.

A. L. B.

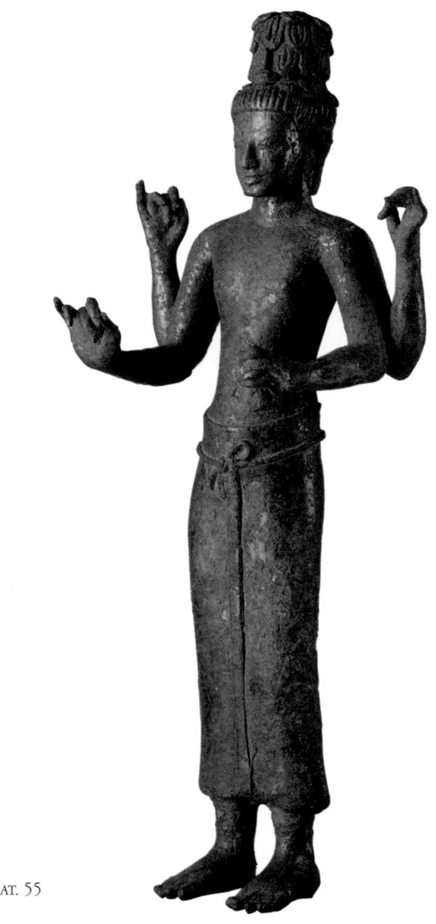

CAT. 55

55

Bodhisattva Maitreya

Thailand, Pre-Angkor, 8th century
Bronze with high silver content; h. 18⅛ in. (46 cm)
Musée Guimet, Paris MA 3321

The bodhisattva Maitreya is presently in the Tushita Heaven (heaven of the satisfied beings), where he teaches the gods whom the Buddha had left behind in order to descend to earth for his reincarnation. He will be the Buddha of the cosmic age to come and, as such, is particularly revered. He is recognizable by the stupa image worn on the front of his hair, which holds the relics of the Buddha Kasyapa. As indicated by his name, Maitreya possesses the *maitri*: the faculty to be benevolent, of a friendly disposition, which has the power to render beings invulnerable.

This bodhisattva may have been part of a triad, forming another bodhisattva's counterpart, flanking a Buddha. This other bodhisattva may have been Avalokiteshvara.

Stylistically, this statuette may be attributed to the second half or the end of the eighth century. It is related to a group of several hundred bronzes found at Prakhon Chai, in a region with a very ancient Khmer population in what is now Thailand. These bronzes are testimony to an important center of Mahayana Buddhist art in this region.

A. L. B.

56

Bodhisattva Avalokiteshvara

Thailand, Pre-Angkor period, 8th century
Bronze; h. 25¼ in. (64 cm)
Musée Guimet, Paris MA 4985

A bodhisattva, or enlightened being, must be portrayed with the perfect appearance of a sixteen-year-old adolescent. In that manner, youthful and smiling, the bodhisattva Avalokiteshvara is here represented as "the master of the ones he rules and protects," according to one of the possible interpretations of his name. He himself is ruled by the esoteric Buddha Amitabha, represented on the front of his elaborately looped hairdo, which prefigures the style of the Angkor period. The costume is simple, since these are his underclothes. The statue would have been dressed and trimmed with real clothes and jewelry in its sanctuary. It has

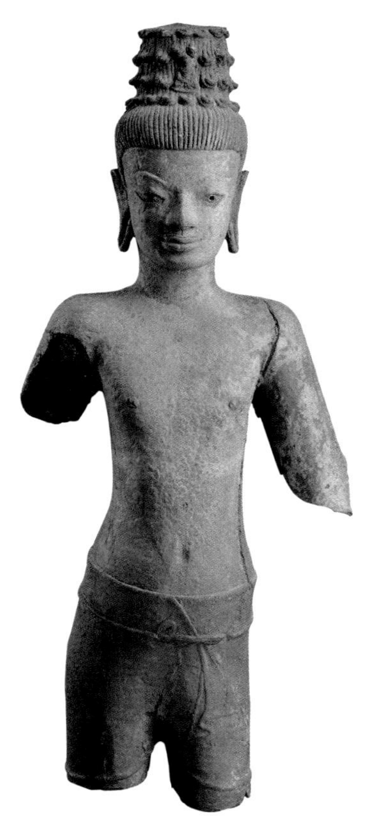

four arms; it is probable that one hand held a lotus bud and another a water vessel.

This Avalokiteshvara was probably part of a triad, standing on one side of a Buddha, with the bodhisattva Maitreya on the other side. Though fragmentary, this statue is related to the tallest sculptures in the Prakhon Chai group known today (only about ten exist). A four-armed Maitreya, such as the one belonging to the Asia Society Galleries or the Maitreya at the Kimbell Art Museum, could be his symmetrical counterpart.

A. L. B.

57

Bodhisattva Avalokiteshvara

Cambodia, Choeung Prey, Phnom Troap
Khleang style, second half of 10th century
Polished gray sandstone; h. 51⅛ in. (130 cm)
Musée Guimet, Paris MG 14909

This sculpture belongs to the official Khleang style, which was very popular in Angkor during the last decades of the tenth century and the early eleventh century.

This Avalokiteshvara is especially interesting because, like many Khmer sculptures, he shows traces of several transformations. The Amitabha Buddha, who originally was represented on the front of the hair, has been recarved to become the *om* syllable, which transformed the Avalokiteshvara into a Shiva, the frontal eye conveniently fitting both. Furthermore, the forearms, of which at least one if not two were stretched outward and held attributes, are missing; the remaining resculptured stumps indicate that metallic forearms had been substituted. Considering the use of metal, and most likely bronze, the statue must have been "converted" at a rather early date; these alterations were probably meant to achieve the transformation of the statue into a Shiva. However, there may also have been a subsequent change of the image into a Buddha or a protective genie.

A. L. B.

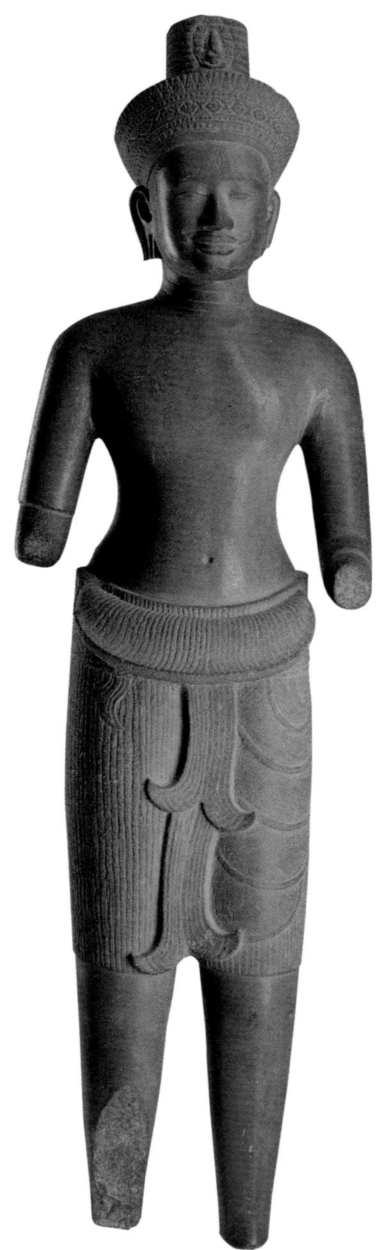

62

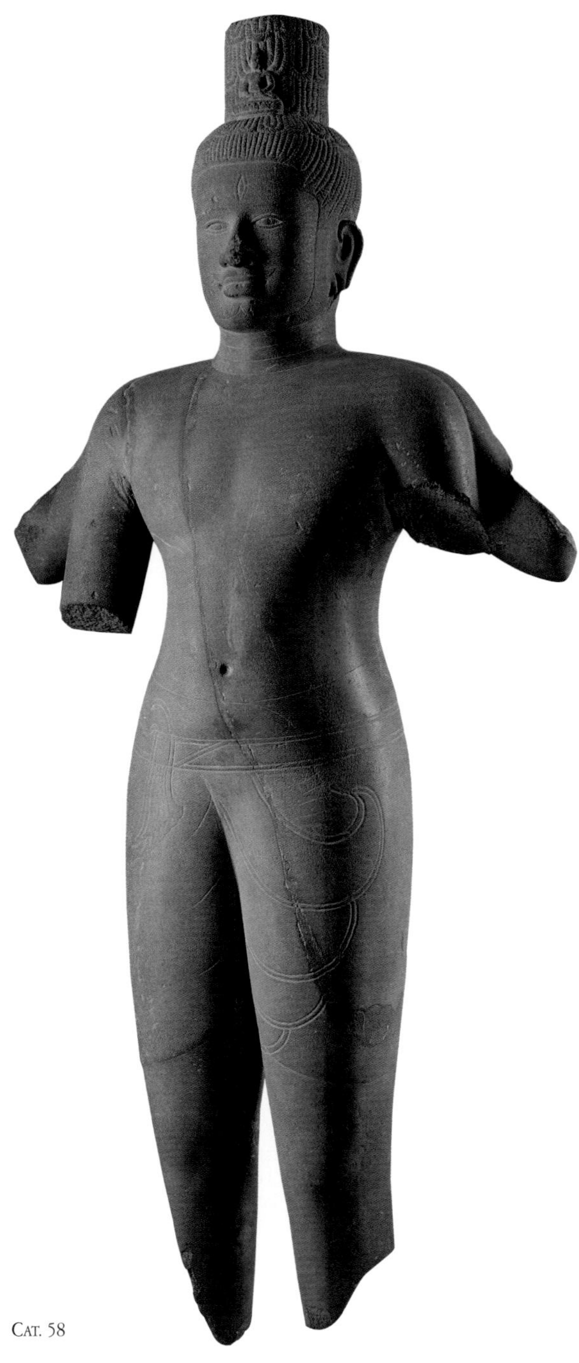

CAT. 58

58

Bodhisattva Avalokiteshvara

Cambodia, Choeung Prey?, Tuol Chi Tep
Banteay Srei style, second half of 10th century
Polished gray sandstone; h. 45⅞ in. (116 cm)
Musée Guimet, Paris MG 14912

Avalokiteshvara is undeniably identifiable by the representation of Jina Amitabha on the front of his bun. This

statue is at present one of the only ones not actually found at Banteay Srei whose style can still be positively identified with that site, due to the innovative aspect of its soft contours and costume. But in Banteay Srei itself, and in another religious perspective (Shivaism), the innovations appear only in the treatment of secondary images (such as male and female door guardians); the cult statues have a traditional appearance. Therefore, even though this is Banteay Srei style, this sculpture was probably carved later, unless this can be explained by the fact—frequently evident in Cambodia—that Buddhist sculpture did not evolve in the same careful manner as Hindu (especially Shivaic) sculpture.

The origin of this piece has never been established with certainty. It is based on an allusive phrase recorded by Etienne Aymonier from his 1882–83 expedition.

A. L. B.

59

Radiating Lokeshvara

Cambodia, Kompong Svay, Preah Khan, Phreah Thkol
Bayon style, end of 12th–early 13th century
Gray sandstone; h. 51⅛ in. (130 cm)
Musée Guimet, Paris MG 18139

Under the reign of Jayavarman VII (1181–1218), as part of a very specific Mahayana Buddhism, the multiple personifications of the bodhisattva Avalokiteshvara became preponderant. The bodhisattva sometimes took on the appearance of an immeasurable entity, on a cosmic scale and inconceivable by the mind: from all pores of his skin emanated rays, at the end of which Buddhas from all universes parallel to ours manifested themselves, more numerous than the grains of sand from the shores of the Ganges.

In this form, the bodhisattva is then called Lokeshvara, the Lord of the Worlds. His shapes are so varied that it is difficult to know with certainty what the attributes are in the eight hands. Multiple images of cosmic Buddhas, all seated in meditation—like the Amitabha on the front of the hair bun with a rosary at its base—entirely cover the torso, arms, and hair. Aside from the Buddhas, eight deities are placed around the waist, in a probable link with the cardinal points, a ninth one appearing on his heart. This cult statue, intended to accompany a high dignitary to the next world and to provide prosperity in this world to the family worshipping it, combines the spirituality of the smiling, meditative

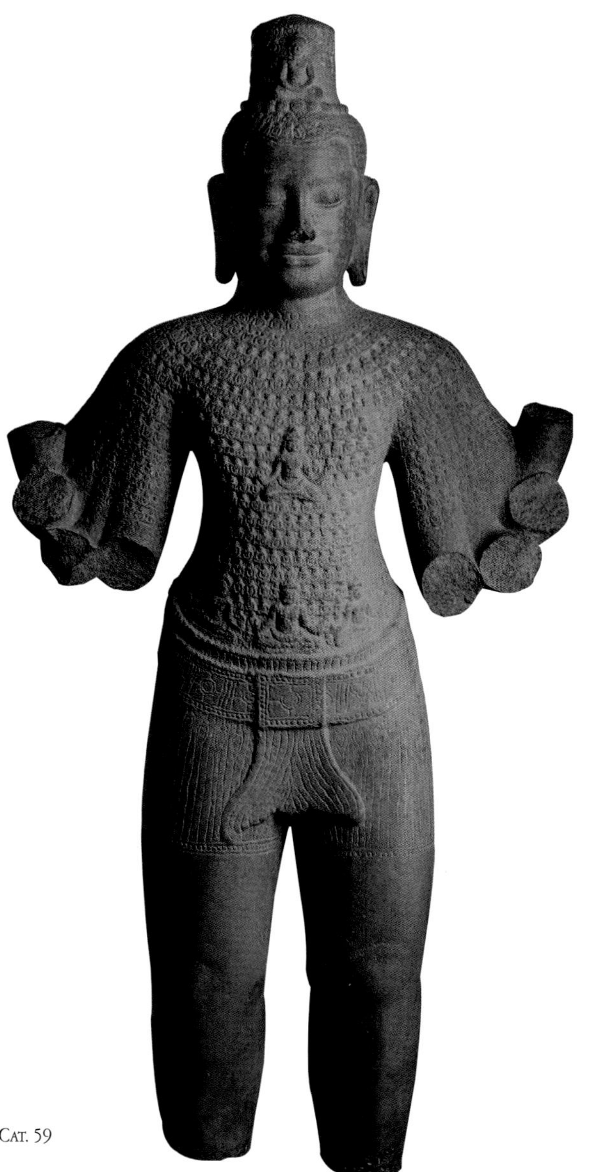

CAT. 59

face and the symbolism of the multiple arms with the humble realism of the body, especially the somewhat heavy legs.

A. L. B.

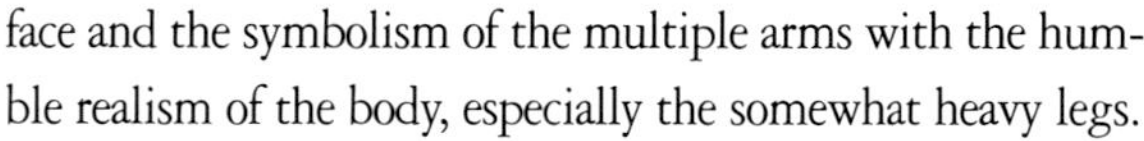

60

Torso of Buddha Seated in Meditation, Sheltered by the Naga

Cambodia, Kompong Svay, Preah Khan
Bayon style, end of 12th–early 13th century
Gray sandstone; h. 43¾ in. (111 cm)
Musée Guimet, Paris MG 18126

In Cambodia, the image of the Buddha meditating, protected by the *naga* (the serpent Muchalinda), is particu-

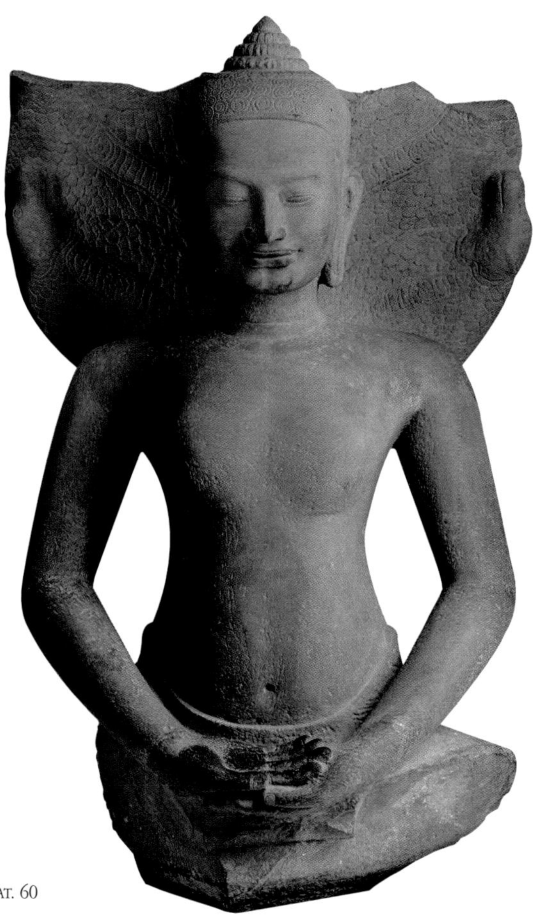

CAT. 60

larly important, even more than in India, because it allows the association of the *naga* (serpent king) and the royal person, the Buddha being the Universal Sovereign within the spiritual domain. However, here it involves tangible forms of a state religion and the origins of Khmer royalty being based on the legend of an alliance: the marriage between the daughter of a *naga* king, owner of the land, and a prince or Brahman who came from India.

The cranial protuberance, masked by a conical *ushnisha*-cover, and the wheel carved in the palm of the visible hand are superhuman marks of the Buddha.

Typical of the Bayon style (the last two decades of the twelfth century and first two decades of the thirteenth century) is this beautiful expression combining inwardness and withdrawal with compassion for all beings, or, expressed in a more Buddhist manner, the loss of passion, the detachment from an illusory world, and the virtue of equanimity toward all animated beings. The restrained contours, while idealizing the human form, also serve to spiritualize it, in contrast to the impersonal and geometrical treatment peculiar to a number of styles of Angkor-period Khmer art preceding the Bayon style.

A. L. B.

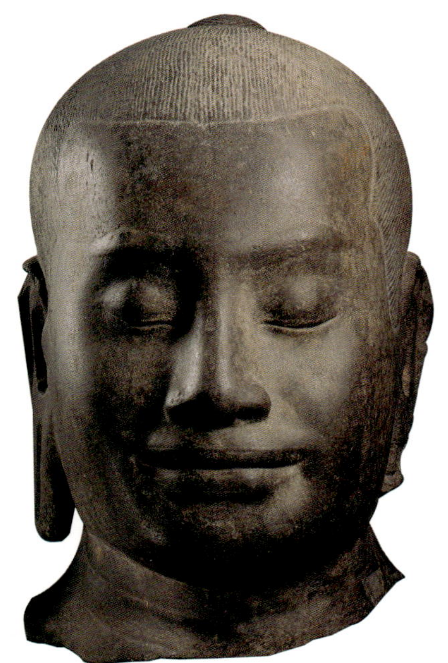

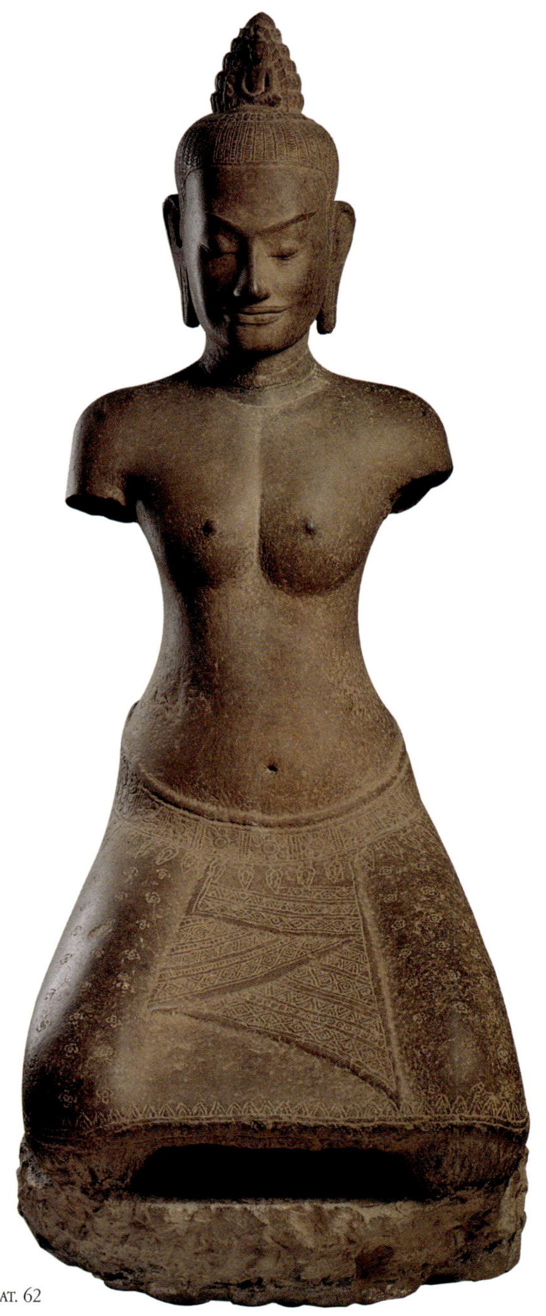

61

Head of Jayavarman VII?

Cambodia, Angkor?
Bayon style, end of 12th–early 13th century
Sandstone (traces of gilding); 15³/₄ in. (40 cm)
Musée Guimet, Paris P 430

In the Mahayana form of Buddhism supported by the state and elaborated by the spiritual masters of Jayavarman VII (r. 1181–1218), the sculptors were able to abandon the abstract ideal of impersonal beauty (the representation of gods and goddesses at the age of sixteen that dominated Shivaic images). It seems that the person of the king himself, but also of the queen and important dignitaries, still more or less idealized, may have served as canon to the artists. Therefore, when the works have been executed by excellent sculptors, we are, as it were, in the presence of "portraits." It always seems, however, that shapes and names were involved that associated the deceased with a divinity, or caused him to be reborn in the "world" of this divinity, which explains why some of these sculptures appear to adopt a worshipping or praying attitude. Apparently, the king himself commissioned his own sculpted portraits during his lifetime, which would explain why fragmentary representations showing him at various ages remain.

Here, Jayavarman VII is represented as an unadorned older man. The king was probably seated with his head bowed, making a gesture of homage to the Supreme Buddha, who protected the Khmer empire.

A. L. B.

62

Kneeling Tara

Cambodia, Angkor, Phreah Khan
Bayon style, end of 12th–early 13th century
Sandstone; h. 43¼ in. (110 cm)
Musée Guimet, Paris MG 18043

This elongated face with rather startling features—the long, straight nose, eyebrows so thick as to look almost made-up, and the frail, almost sickly body—may very well represent Jayarajadevi, the first wife of Jayavarman VII.

After her death, her older sister Indradevi, who in turn became queen, had commissioned statues for her, as well as for the king. The deepened groove between the poorly developed breasts indicates that the arms must have been stretched forward, hands close together in a gesture of homage or offering. The conical bun cover carries, in front, the image of the Jina Amitabha, indicating that the deceased goddess had joined Tara's world or had become an aspect of Tara, the consort of bodhisattva Avalokiteshvara.

This statue, with its intense expression of spirituality, is, without doubt, one of the most beautiful ever to see the light during the period of Mahayana Buddhism under Jayavarman VII.

A. L. B.

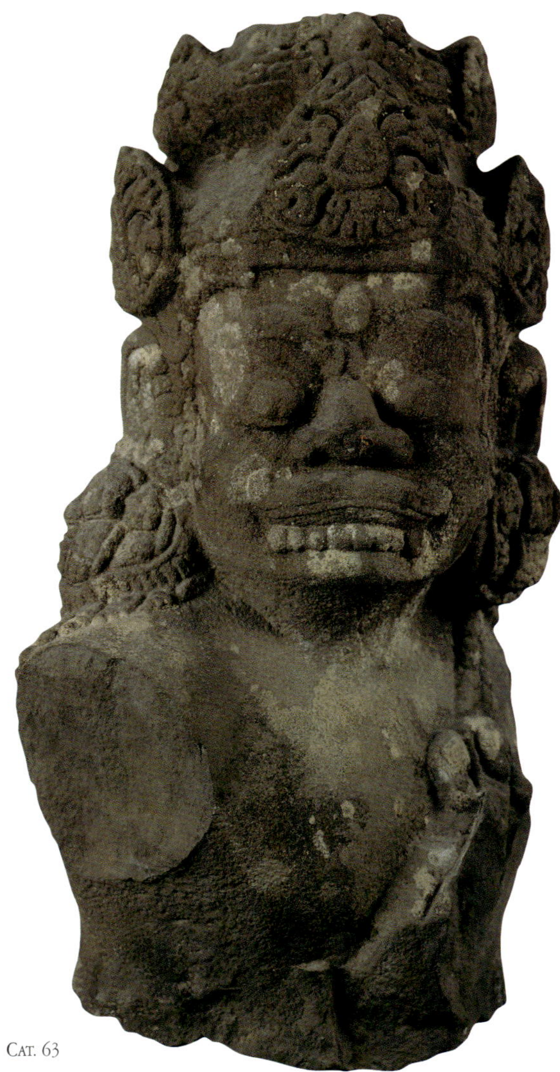

63

Bust of Dvarapala
Vietnam (ancient Champa), Quang Nam Da Nang,
Dong-duong style, c. 875–915
Sandstone; h. 26 in. (66 cm)
Musée Guimet, Paris MA 3776

The huge Buddhist foundation of Dong-duong (today the Quang Nam Da Nang province of Vietnam, which was formerly the Amaravati province of the ancient coastal kingdom of Champa) is the main work of one ruler, Indravarman II, who seems to have seized power in Indrapura "not because he inherited the monarchy from his grandfather or father, but solely through destiny and the merits acquired during numerous preceding existences" (according to the inscription from the foundation stele, dated 875 A.D.).

In Dong-duong, at the end of a very long roadway, the buildings are spaced out among four successive surrounding walls, each entrance guarded by two Dvarapala (door guardians) whose fierce aspect is supposed to ward off evil influences; this piece is a fragment from the most remote wall. The Dvarapala are very representative of the "Dong-duong style," which, in statuary, exaggerates the tendencies of the preceding style. This suits their nature as terrible beings, with their knitted brows, bulging eyes, and protruding fangs. The adornment consists of three-headed *naga* worn as a Brahmanic cord or as earrings. The heavy and generous lines of the foliated scrolls constituting the tiara's fleurons are characteristic of the style and can be found in the decorations of pilasters and buildings.

A. L. B.

64

Jina Aksobhya
Indonesia, central Java, 9th century
Andesite; h. 40⅛ in. (102 cm)
On loan from the Musée de l'Homme, 1930
Musée Guimet, Paris MG 18246

In the advanced form of Mahayana Buddhism observed in Indonesia during the central Java period, and especially in Borobudur, esoteric "meditation" Buddhas, sometimes called jina ("conquerors"), formed a pseudo-pantheon of apparitional "divinities" visible only to the bodhisattvas. Their iconography seems to be based on certain great moments in the life of the human Buddha, Shakyamuni, and they are structured according to a strict hierarchy. Thus, Aksobhya, "the Immovable One," corresponds to the moment when the future Buddha, attacked by Mara (the god of Death), calls the earth as a witness by lightly touching it with the fingertips of his right hand.

In the art of central Java, representations entirely sculpted in the round were later replaced by high reliefs set off against a stele, in this piece also serving as a flamboyant halo. Here, Aksobhya is wearing only the monastic robe, leaving the right shoulder bare. He is sitting cross-legged, with only the sole of the right foot visible, on a lotus in full bloom. His right hand rests on his knee in a position evoking the *bhumisparshamudra* ("gesture as if to touch the earth") of the future Buddha Shakyamuni.

A. L. B.

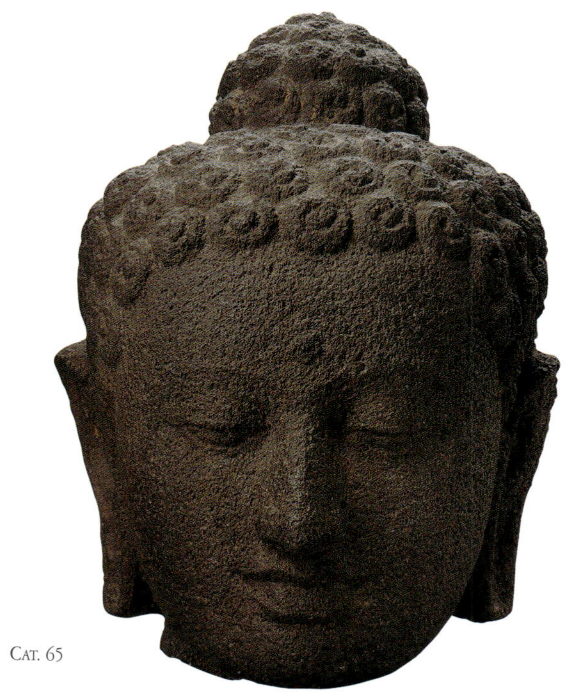

Cat. 65

65

Head of a Buddha

Indonesia, central Java, c. 800
Andesite; h. 12⅝ in. (32 cm)
Musée Guimet, Paris MA 2514

This type head resembles the heads of the jinas of Borobudur, carved in the round: wide face, serene and majestic, in the spirit of the Indian works of the post-Gupta and Pala periods. The *ushnisha* is well indicated and covered with large locks, all coiled toward the right, as is the rest of the hair. The forehead carries the *urna*, also represented like a lock, but smaller. This is probably a representation not of the historical Buddha but of one of the jinas of Mahayana Buddhism.

A. L. B.

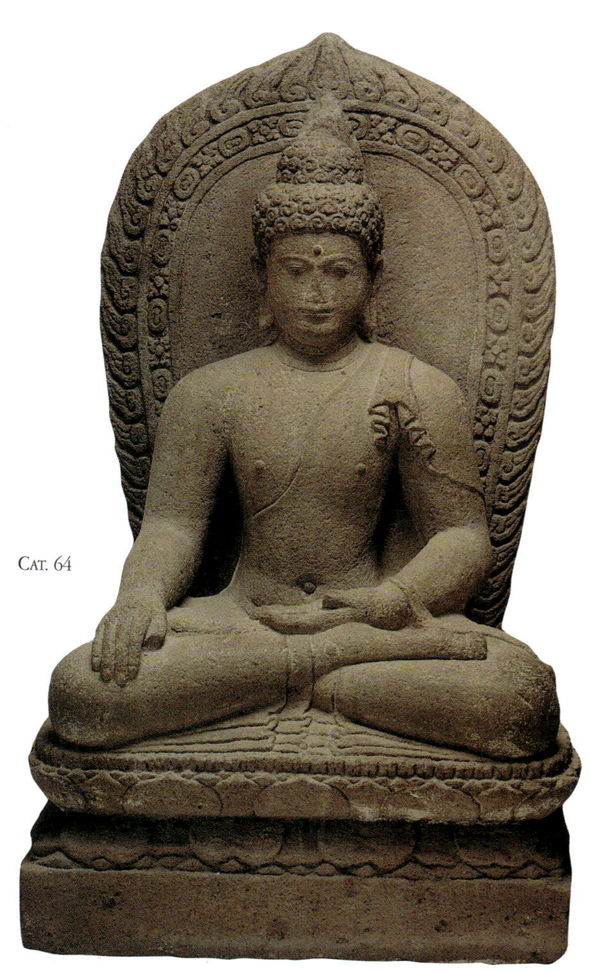

Cat. 64

66

Bodhisattva Lokeshvara

Indonesia, central Java, c. 9th century
Bronze; h. 13⅜ in. (34 cm)
Musée Guimet, Paris MG 3816

This very famous Mahayana piece represents bodhisattva Lokeshvara, or Avalokiteshvara, appearing in a super-

67

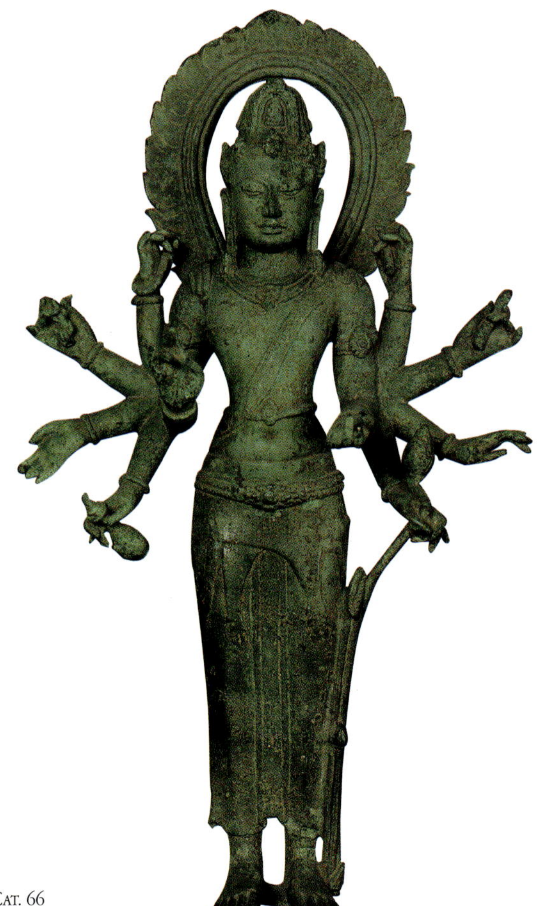

human form with ten arms, which is very rarely depicted. The bodhisattva is easily identifiable because the image of the Jina Amitabha, the "leader of his lineage," appears on the front of his bun shaped out of hair locks. The gestures made by the two "main" hands should probably not be interpreted as separate *mudra*, but the two together form a variation of the teaching or reasoning gesture. The attributes or gestures of the remaining hands are, from top to bottom, starting with his right hands: the rosary, the lacing twine, the gesture of giving, and the water jar; in his left hands: the book, a broken object that may be an elephant hook or the triple staff, the gesture of reassurance, and a lotus stalk. As behooves a deity, the bodhisattva is surrounded by a flaming halo, and, as a prince, wears the Brahmanic cord and a rich but light gold jewelry piece. The bodhisattva wears a tiger skin around the hips, above his long garment, thus showing the influence of the Shivaic iconography on Mahayana Buddhism, an influence that was especially strong in Indonesia.

This bronze is truly exceptional in spite of its small dimensions, and is one of the most beautiful of all those now known from ancient Indonesia. The modeling, proportions, and balance of the composition are all admirable.

A. L. B.

67

Bodhisattva

Indonesia, central Java, 9th–10th century
Bronze, 4⅜ in. (11 cm)
Musée Guimet, Paris MG 3824

This enigmatic bodhisattva forms part of a group of three works in the Guimet collection, which share the same characteristics: they are sitting in the same position (*satvaparayanka*, right leg placed on top of left leg), the left hand is placed palm upward on the knee, the right hand presents an attribute, and they are not placed on their original pedestals. They may have been part of the same mandala, but the reference to Indian texts keeps their identity uncertain. Here, the attributes are the book (*pustaka*) placed on the blue lotus (*nilotpala*), which makes us think of Manjushri as well as an aspect of Vajragarbha (Vajrapani), endowed with the blue lotus and the Book of the Ten Earths.

A. L. B.

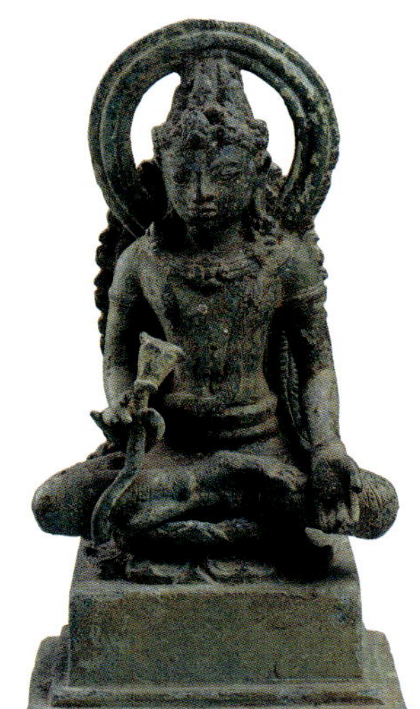

68

Jambhala

Indonesia, central Java, 9th–10th century
Bronze; h. 11 in. (28 cm)
Musée Guimet, Paris MG 3814

Jambhala, the god of wealth, seems to have been especially venerated in Java, a kingdom where trade was highly regarded. Seated on a pillow in the relaxed position (*lalitasana*), his dangling foot kicking over a vase from which

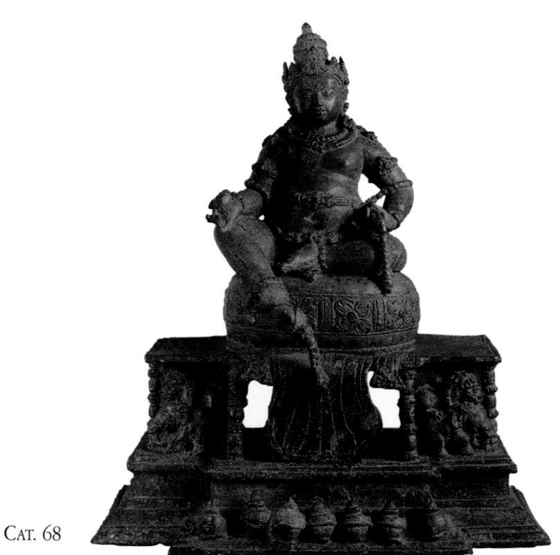

Cat. 68

jewels pour forth, the abundantly decorated, rather chubby god presents a fruit in his right hand (*jambara*, citron, a fruit whose symbolism of abundance is analogous to the pomegranate in Mediterranean mythology), and clutches in his left hand the neck of a mongoose spitting out jewels. Other pots of jewels probably evoke the Eight Treasures (*astanidhi*) at Jambhala's disposal. The proof that Jambhala was considered to be an important god lies in the composition of the pedestal: the elephant motif symbolizes the earth, and the lion is a solar and royal symbol. The Sanskrit formula said to be the Buddhist creed is engraved at the back of the pedestal: "What concerns the things brought on by a cause, the Tathagata has indicated their cause and [the Way to follow to bring about] their cessation; thus the Great Ascetic Being has spoken."

A. L. B.

69

Vairocana

Indonesia, end of central Java period–early east Java period,
10th century
Bronze, dark green patina; h. 6⅛ in. (15.5 cm)
Musée Guimet, Paris MG 18290

Vairocana is the esoteric Buddha, or jina, associated with the zenith, his name referring to the brightness and glow of the solar rays. Together with other superior entities of the Mahayana, Vairocana usually stands in the center of a mandala, composed of a certain number of lower ranked entities who belong to his "family" and turn toward him to revere him.

Here, wearing the monastic robe, he is seated in a meditative position on a lotus in full bloom (*padmasana*) and forms with both hands a specific *mudra*, the *bodhyangamudra*. In earlier sculptures from Borobudur (ninth century), Vairocana makes the traditional gesture for putting into motion the Wheel of the Law (*dharmachakramudra*). In this later work, as indicated by certain stylistic and technical details, the *bodhyangamudra* is made by the five fingers of the right hand clutching the raised index finger of the left hand; this *mudra* is also found in Japanese Buddhism. There, the raised index finger is the world of animated beings, protected by the world of the five cosmic Buddhas; or the five fingers may correspond to the five elements that are the sense organs, while the index finger is the mind (*manas*), at the same time served and harmed by the senses; or, finally, it may be the symbolic representation of the union of the Upaya (the index finger, the male element) and the Prajna (wisdom, the female element), who together produce the thought of enlightenment.

A. L. B.

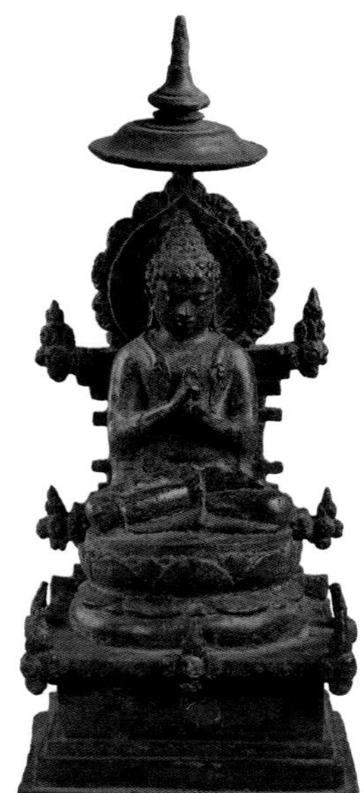

Cat. 69

70

Standing Buddha

Burma, 14th century
Wood, lacquered with traces of gilding;
h. 73⅝ in. (187 cm)
Musée Guimet, Paris MA 3795

This work is related to numerous statues of the Buddha, also carved in a tree trunk and approximately full-size, which were found in Burma, in the various temples of Pagan. Following the capture and pillage of Pagan by the hanging alongside his body, the hand making the gesture for giving (*varamudra*). The fact that the Buddha is decorated with royal ornaments conforms to the Indian Mahayana tradition, one of the sources of ancient Burmese art.

A. L. B.

71

Head of a Crowned Buddha
Thailand, Ayutthaya, 15th–16th century
Bronze; h. 17¾ in. (45 cm)
Musée Guimet, Paris EO 1622

The Theravada Buddhist art of Thailand is renowned for the mastery with which its artists specialized in bronzes rendering the Buddha's superhuman image. During the Ayutthaya period, fluid contours have given way to other qualities, more graphic than plastic, leading to a geometrical stylization that is very refined in ancient works such as this one, but which in later centuries will become more and more simplified in form and elaborate in decor. As is the case here, the Buddha is often represented wearing royal finery, the Thai tradition, being based on texts that explain that Buddha could have taken the appearance of beings he wanted to convert, and among these beings, a great king who despised begging monks. Originally this bronze was probably gilded, with some details inlaid.

A. L. B.

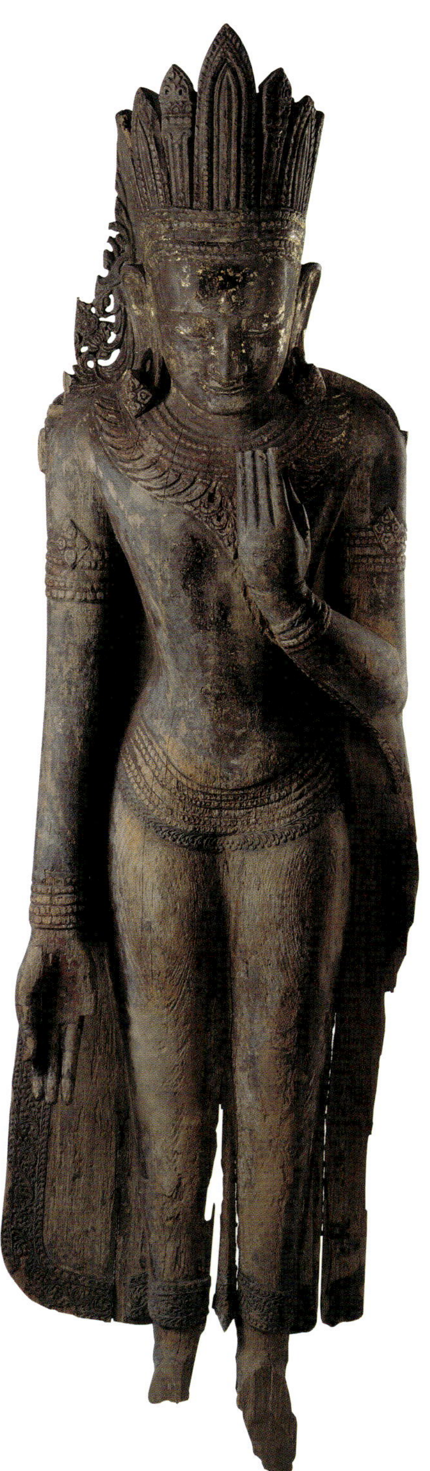

Cat. 70

Mongols in 1287, the sanctuary still remained active even though the country was politically weakened and divided. These Buddhas, whose style seems to be a continuation of the monuments of Pagan's period of glory (c. 1050–1298), are probably the most ancient remnants of an art form that is represented mostly by very late examples from the Mandalay period (nineteenth century).

The Buddha wears the monastic robe, holding the tail end in his left hand pressed against his chest, the right arm

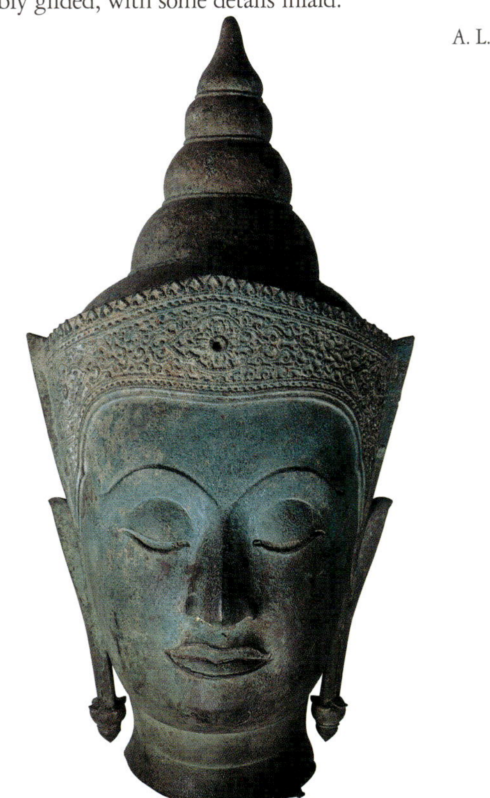

Cat. 71

Selected Bibliography

Akiyama, Terukazu, and S. Matsubara. *Buddhist Cave Temples, New Researches*. Vol. 2 of *Arts of China*. Palo Alto: Kodansha, 1969.

Allchin, F. R., and Norman Hammond, eds. *The Archaeology of Afghanistan from Earliest Times to the Timurid Period*. New York: Academic Press, 1978.

Along the Ancient Silk Routes: Central Asian Art from the West Berlin State Museums. New York: Metropolitan Museum of Art, 1982.

Auboyer, Jeannine. Introduction to *Rarities of the Musée Guimet*. New York: Asia Society, 1974.

Béguin, Gilles. "A propos d'une tiare d'officiant bouddhique." *La Revue du Louvre* 3 (1984): 176–83.

———. "Bronzes himalayens." *La Revue du Louvre* 4–5 (1974): 333–36.

———. *L'Inde et le monde indianisé au musée national des arts asiatiques-Guimet*. Paris: Réunion des musées nationaux, 1992.

———. "Two himalayen bronzes in the Guimet Museum." *East and West* 26 (1976): 167.

Buddhist Sculptures from Mid-Eleventh to the End of Twelfth Centuries. Kyoto: Kyoto National Museum, 1991.

Cambon, Pierre. *Paris-Tokyo-Begram: Hommage à Joseph Hackin, 1886-1941*. Paris: Editions Recherche sur les civilisations, 1986.

Casey, Jane Anne, ed. *Medieval Sculpture from Eastern India: Selections from the Nalin Collection*. Livingston: Nalini International Publications, 1985.

Chandra, Moti. *Stone Sculpture in the Prince of Wales Museum*. Bombay: Prince of Wales Museum of Western India, 1974.

Chandra, Pramod. *The Sculpture of India: 3000 B.C.–1300 A.D.* Washington: National Gallery of Art, 1985.

Chinese Buddhist Sculpture from the Wei through the T'ang Dynasties. Taiwan: National Museum of History, 1983.

Choi, Sunu. *Five Thousand Years of Korean Art*. Seoul: Hyonam, 1979.

Chutiwongs, Nandana, and Denise Patry Leidy. *Buddha of the Future: An Early Maitreya from Thailand*. New York: Asia Society Galleries, 1994.

The Crucible of Compassion and Wisdom: Special Exhibition Catalogue of the Buddhist Bronzes from the Nitta Group Collection at the National Palace Museum. Tokyo: National Palace Museum, 1987.

Czuma, Stanislaw J. *Kushan Sculpture: Images from Early India*. Cleveland: Cleveland Museum of Art, 1985.

Denès, Françoise. *Les Bois de Dunhuang au Musée Guimet*. Paris: Editions des musées nationaux, 1976.

Desai, Vishakha, and Darielle Mason. *Gods, Guardians, and Lovers*. New York: Asia Society Galleries, 1993.

Desroches, Jean-Paul. *Asie Extrême: Chine, Corée, Japon, Viêtnam*. Paris: Réunion des musées nationaux, 1993.

Felton, Wolfgang, and Martin Lerner. *Thai and Cambodian Sculpture from the Sixth to the Fourteenth Centuries*. London: Philip Wilson, 1989.

Fisher, Robert E. *Buddhist Art and Architecture*. London: Thames and Hudson, 1993.

Fontein, Jan. *The Sculpture of Indonesia*. Washington: National Gallery of Art, 1990.

Foucher, Alfred C. *The Beginnings of Buddhist Art*. Trans. L. A. and F. W. Thomas. Paris: Geuthner, 1918.

Gaulier, Simone, Robert Jera-Bezard, and Monique Maillard. *Buddhism in Afghanistan and Central Asia*. Leiden: Brill, 1976.

Gupte, Ramesh S. *Iconography of the Hindus, Buddhists, and Jains*. 2nd edition. Bombay: Taraporevala, 1980.

Hackin, Joseph. *Guide-Catalogue du Musée Guimet: Les collections bouddhiques*. Paris: Van Oest, 1923.

Harle, Joseph C. *The Art and Architecture of the Indian Subcontinent*. New York: Penguin, 1990.

———. *Gupta Sculpture: Indian Sculpture of the Fourth to Sixth Centuries A.D.* New York: Oxford University Press, 1974.

Harris, Victor, and Ken Matsushima. *Kamakura: The Renaissance of Japanese Sculpture, 1185–1333*. British Museum Press, 1991.

Huntington, Susan L. *The Art of Ancient India: Buddhist, Hindu, Jain*. New York: Weatherhill, 1985.

Huntington, Susan L., and John C. Huntington. *Leaves from the Bodhi Tree*. Seattle and London: Dayton Art Institute and University of Washington Press, 1990.

Ingholt, Harald. *Gandharan Art in Pakistan*. New York: Pantheon, 1957.

Kim, Won-yong. *Art and Archaeology of Ancient Korea*. Seoul: Taekwang, 1986.

Klimburg-Salter, Deborah E. *The Kingdom of Bamiyan: Buddhist Art and Culture of the Hindu Kush*. Naples: Istituto universitario orientale, Dipartimento di studi asiatici; Rome: Istituto italiano per il medio ed estremo oriente, 1989.

———. *The Silk Route and the Diamond Path: Esoteric Buddhist Art on the Trans-Himalayan Trade Routes*. Los Angeles: UCLA Art Council, 1982.

Le Bonheur, Albert. "Angkor et le pays khmer ancien." *Dossiers Histoire et Archéologie (Archeologia)*, no. 125 (March 1988): 22–27.

———. *Cambodge: Angkor, Temples en péril*. Paris: Herscher, 1989.

———. *Des dieux, des rois, et des hommes: Bas-reliefs d'Angkor Vat et du Bàyon (Cambodge, XIIe siècle)*. Exposition de photographies de M. Joroslav Poncar et al. au Musée Guimet. Geneva: Editions Olizane; London: 1995.

———. "La vie quotidienne d'après les bas-reliefs du Bayon." *Dossiers Histoire et Archéologie (Archeologia)*, no. 125 (March 1988): 72–83.

Lee, Sherman E. *A History of Far Eastern Art*. 5th ed. New York: Abrams, 1994.

Lee Jung, Hee. "The Origins and Development of the Pensive Bodhisattva Images of Asia." *Artibus Asiae* 53 (1993): 311–53.

Leidy, Denise Patry. *Treasures of Asian Art: The Asia Society's Mr. and Mrs. John D. Rockefeller 3rd Collection*. New York: Asia Society Galleries and Abbeville Press, 1994.

Lerner, Martin. *The Flame and the Lotus: Indian and Southeast Asian Art from the Kronos Collections*. New York: Abrams, 1984.

Lerner, Martin, and Steven Kossak. "The Arts of South and Southeast Asia." *Metropolitan Museum of Art Bulletin*, vol. 51, no. 4 (spring 1994).

Mizuno, Seiichi. *Chinese Stone Sculpture*. Tokyo: Mayuyama, 1950.

Musée national des arts asiatiques-Guimet. Paris: Beaux Arts Hors Serie / Réunion des musées nationaux, 1993.

Nishikawa, Kyotaro, and Emily J. Sano. *The Great Age of Japanese Buddhist Sculpture, A.D. 600–1300*. Fort Worth: Kimbell Art Museum; New York: Japan Society, 1982.

Old Masks: Religion and Performing Arts. Kyoto: Kyoto National Museum, 1980.

Pal, Pratapaditya. *Art of the Himalayas: Treasures from Nepal and Tibet*. New York: Hudson Hills, 1991.

———. *Art of Nepal*. Los Angeles: Los Angeles County Museum of Art; Berkeley: University of California Press, 1985.

———. *Art of Tibet*. Los Angeles: Los Angeles County Museum of Art; Berkeley: University of California Press, 1983.

———, ed. *Asian Art: Selections from the Norton Simon Museum*. Reprinted from *Orientations*, July 1988. Pasadena: Norton Simon Museum, 1988.

———. *The Ideal Image: The Gupta Sculptural Tradition and Its Influence*. New York: Asia Society, 1978.

———. *Indian Sculpture*. 2 vols. Los Angeles: Los Angeles County Museum of Art; Berkeley: University of California Press, 1986.

———. *Light of Asia: Buddha Sakyamuni in Asian Art*. Los Angeles: Los Angeles County Museum of Art, 1984.

———. *The Sensuous Immortals: A Selection of Sculptures from the Pan-Asian Collection*. Los Angeles: Los Angeles County Museum of Art, 1977.

Rosenfield, John M. *The Dynastic Arts of the Kushans*. Berkeley: University of California Press, 1967.

Sérinde, terre de Bouddha: Dix siècles d'art sur la route de la Soie. Paris: Réunion des musées nationaux, 1995.

Sugiyama, Jiro. *Classic Buddhist Sculpture: The Tempyo Period*. New York: Kodansha, 1982.

Tokyo National Museum. *Sculpture*. Vol. 3 of *Pageant of Japanese Art*. Tokyo: Toto Bunka, 1953.

Whitfield, Roderick, and Anne Farrer. *Caves of the Thousand Buddhas: Chinese Art from the Silk Route*. London: British Museum, 1990.

Williams, Joanna Gottfried. *The Art of Gupta India: Empire and Province*. Princeton: Princeton University Press, 1982.

Zwalf, W., ed. *Buddhism: Art and Faith*. London: British Museum, 1985